INTRODUCTION TO ISLAMIC LAW

Introduction to
ISLAMIC LAW

Principles of Civil, Criminal,
and International Law
under the *Shari'a*

Jonathan G. Burns

JuraLaw

INTRODUCTION TO ISLAMIC LAW:
Principles of Civil, Criminal, and
International Law under the *Shari'a*

ISBN (13): 978-0-9845182-5-8
ISBN (10): 0-9845182-5-8

JuraLaw™
an imprint of TellerBooks™
TellerBooks.com/JuraLaw

www.TellerBooks.com

Manufactured in the U.S.A.

For Mom and Dad, with much love

ABBREVIATED CONTENTS

DETAILED CONTENTS

FOREWORD

The globe at the moment has become a huge village. Today, Muslims and non-Muslims live side by side and must know and learn about one another, enjoying shared commonalities while tolerating and respecting differences. Having taught law in both Egypt and the United States and having lectured at many conferences around the globe, I have found that significant confusion and misunderstanding exists between Muslims and non-Muslims alike regarding different cultural, religious, and ideological norms and beliefs.

Particularly in the Western world, however, Islamic law (*Shari'a*) is a subject that is so often misinterpreted and misunderstood, thought to be a group of oppressive rules and unfair standards which are biased, discriminatory, and backward, opposing and affronting contemporary notions of human dignity and contradicting human rights values and norms.

The truth, however, is quite otherwise. Philosophies of equality and justice inspire the rules of *usual al-fiqh* (Islamic jurisprudence) and are applicable to both individuals and to the affairs of the entire Muslim community, which is designed, stratified, and firmly sheltered by Islamic legal norms and *Shari'a* tracks. In addition, the *Shari'a*'s spirit, which originates from divine revelation, exemplifies global and universal principles of dignity, equity, social justice, and human solidarity. Indeed, the non-Muslim reader will be surprised by the great similarity of specific legal perspectives between *Shari'a* law and positive (Western) law in cases of, for instance, the protection of the family, criminal law and criminal justice, property law, banking and financial systems, laws relating to elderly and handicapped individuals, and international law.

Thus, it is very important – particularly in non-Muslim nations – to have objective and educated sources of scholarship that provide truth and clarity where misunderstanding and fear pervades. I am delighted to say that this book – an outstanding and impressive contribution to Islamic scholarship authored by my friend and former student, Jonathan Burns – helps to provide such clarity. This book, *Introduction to Islamic Law*, is not an inclusive treatise but a succinct, clear, and captivating summary of the basic principles of Islamic law which are applicable to the Muslim *Ummah* (community) in general.

I am confident that readers will wholeheartedly enjoy this exposition and acquire significant academic benefits from reading it. With great pleasure, therefore, I highly recommend *Introduction to Islamic Law* to scholars, non-Muslims, and any individual who desires to learn and know about the *Shari'a* rules and its basic values through an objective, rational medium.

Mohamed A. 'Arafa, Ph.D.
Assistant and Adjunct Professor of Law
Alexandria University Faculty of Law, Egypt
Indiana University Robert H. McKinney School of Law

ACKNOWLEDGEMENTS

It is nearly impossible to achieve any degree of success without the support of friends, family, colleagues, and role models. Constantly, I am amazed at the selflessness of highly successful people in my life who have stooped low and made themselves vulnerable in order to help me to achieve.

First, many thanks are due to my mentor and friend John M. B. Balouziyeh, Esq. for making this book possible. John's interactions with me from the moment we met can only be described as utterly selfless and I aspire to, one day, rise to the level of his character, experience, and intellect.

Further, I am extremely grateful to my friend and former professor Mohamed A. 'Arafa, Ph.D. for taking the time to contribute the foreword for this book, undertaking a final review of the manuscript, and providing excellent scholarly clarification and advice to ensure its accuracy.

I would also like to thank Amgad T. Husein, Esq., managing partner of Dentons in Riyadh, for arranging my visit to the Kingdom of Saudi Arabia, the heartland of Islam, where I was able to observe firsthand the application of Islamic law within the context of international transactions and finance in a *Shari'a* jurisdiction.

Additionally, I would like to thank Robert D. Cheesebourough, Esq. for allowing me several years ago to work as an intern in his law office, taking me under his wing as a mentor, and inspiring me to attend law school and pursue a legal career.

Finally, I cannot begin to express the gratitude that is due to my loving family for their undying support and encouragement. Thank you all.

~ Jonathan G. Burns

Preliminary Notes

All Arabic words – except names of persons – are transliterated into the English language and italicized.

All references to Quranic passages are derived from THE HOLY QUR'AN (Saheeh International, Dar Abul-Qasim Publishing, 1997).

It is appropriate and often expected in Islamic tradition to always refer to Muhammad as "the Prophet Muhammad" in both speech and writing. Further, other prophetic figures in Jewish, Christian, and Islamic history should be referred to with their appropriate titles, as well (*e.g.*, the Prophet Moses, the Prophet Jesus, etc.). In addition, it is respectful and customary to follow each spoken or written occurrence of influential figures in Islamic history with an honorific phrase, such as "peace be upon him," or a corresponding acronym, such as "PBUH." However, the constant use of such titles, phrases, and acronyms in written works tends to slow down and hamper the reading process. Thus, the Prophet Muhammad (PBUH) is generally referred to throughout this book as "Muhammad" and other prophets within the Muslim tradition are referenced by only their names (*e.g.*, "Jesus") in order to save space in the manuscript and time in the reading process.

CHAPTER 1. OVERVIEW: FOUNDATIONS OF ISLAMIC LAW (*SHARI'A*)

A. WHAT IS ISLAM?

The root word for the word "Islam" in Arabic is "*sa-la-ma*," which means "submission." As such, the overriding principle of the religion of Islam is submission to Allah (God). Submitting one's life to God is effected by adhering to His commands. Most Muslim scholars and adherents from all walks of life agree on five basic divine commands that, together, form the core of the Islamic faith. The "Five Pillars of Islam" are the *Shahada*, prayer, *Zakat*, fasting, and the *Hajj*.

1. The *Shahada*

First, the *Shahada* is called the inseparable testimony of Islam. It is the underpinning of the Islamic faith and must be recited by a person with sincerity in order for her to be counted amongst the followers of Islam. That is, an unthinking chant of the *Shahada* without a genuine belief in the truth of its contents will not do. While there is no formulaic recitation that satisfies the requirements of the *Shahada*, most scholars agree that the following statement is sufficient: "There is no god but Allah and Muhammad is His prophet."

2. Prayer

Second, most scholars agree that Islam generally requires adherents to perform five daily prayers at five different times during the day. The prayers occur at dawn, at noon, in the afternoon, at dusk, and at night. Muslims must purify themselves by washing prior to prayer. Further, they must perform their prayers in a pure spot facing towards Mecca.

3. *Zakat*

Third, payment of *Zakat* is a strict requirement in Islam (*see infra* Chapter Three). In Arabic, *Zakat* means "to purify or develop" and is often referred to as almsgiving or charity. However, this definition is deceiving because *Zakat* is a mandatory tax. It is literally a legal right held by the poor against those who are not poor. The *Zakat* is collected on income received during one lunar year. Generally, scholars agree that the *Zakat* is calculated at 2.5 percent of any cash income, 5 to 10 percent of any agricultural income, and 20 percent of any income received by extracting natural resources or minerals from the earth.

4. Fasting

Fourth, fasting is another Pillar of Islam. Fasting is considered by many to be an effective means of reminding Muslims of their human frailty, the need for God's provision, and the misery of the poor. As such, Muslims individually may engage in fasts on many occasions. However, fasting during the holy month of Ramadan is generally an obligatory act for all Muslims. On the *Hijri* calendar, Ramadan is the ninth month, during which the *Qur'an* was revealed to the Prophet Muhammad (PBUH). As such, God specifically set apart the month of Ramadan as a time for fasting.[1] During Ramadan, Muslims refrain from eating, drinking, smoking,

---

[1] "The month of Ramadan [is that] in which was revealed the *Qur'an*, a guidance for the people and clear proofs of guidance and criterion. So whoever sights [the new moon of] the month, let him fast it; and whoever is ill or on a journey - then an equal number of other days. Allah intends for you ease and does not intend for you hardship and [wants] for you to complete the period and to glorify Allah for that [to] which He has guided you; and perhaps you will be grateful." *Qur'an* 2:185

and engaging in sexual activity from sunrise until sunset. However, strict adherence to this Pillar is not required from those for whom fasting would be dangerous or extremely unbearable, including children, the physically ill, the elderly, pregnant women, and travelers.

5. The *Hajj*

The fifth and final Pillar of Islam is the *Hajj*. Prior to the revelation of the *Qur'an* to Muhammad, Mecca was a cultural, commercial, and religious melting pot. The *Ka'aba* was at the center of Mecca and was home to many idols representing pagan gods. Worshippers of these gods would make a yearly pilgrimage to the *Ka'aba* out of a religious duty. Muhammad was born and resided in Mecca and, early in the birth of Islam, faced persecution from the Meccan people for his beliefs and public statements. Thereafter, Muhammad and his few followers fled to Medina, where Islam was largely accepted by its inhabitants. With a large, impassioned, and powerful following, Muhammad later returned to Mecca, converted most of its inhabitants to Islam, destroyed the pagan idols at the *Ka'aba*, and declared the *Ka'aba* to be thenceforth the house of the one true God. All physically and financially able Muslims are required to make the pilgrimage to the *Ka'aba* in Mecca at least once during their lifetime.

While Islam is a diverse religion with many different interpretations, sects, and viewpoints, its fundamental principle that is observed by all true Muslims is submission to God. Without prejudice to each one of these diverse beliefs under the large umbrella of Islam, the Five Pillars of Islam comprise the basic underpinning of the Islamic religion, submission to God.

B. WHAT IS ISLAMIC LAW?

1. Introduction

Islamic law and *Shari'a* are interchangeable terms used to describe the correct standard of living according to adherents of the religion of Islam. The word "*shari'a*" literally means "road" in the Arabic language and even shares the same root as the Arabic "*shari'*," meaning "street." However, "*shari'a*" traditionally referred to a well-worn path traversed by camels through the desert that led to a source of water, a scarce and precious resource. As such, the word "*Shari'a*" (as a proper noun) came to be known as mankind's pathway to salvation through the inhospitable, perilous, and harsh desert of life.

The law abhors a vacuum. In the same sense, the *Shari'a* is a global concept that is able to answer every moral, legal, religious, or other question. With this in mind, it is important to note that the *Shari'a* can be divided into two duties, which together encompass the whole duty of man. The first duty involves mankind's relationship with God. In other words, the duty is worship to Allah and is, thus, a duty that is owed to God alone. The second duty involves mankind's relations with each other. Interestingly, the majority of Islamic law is in reference to the first duty, mankind's relationship with God. The second duty, justice in transactions with mankind, refers to what legal practitioners would call "law," including contractual relationships, tortious conduct, taxation, and so on. Because this is a book designed for the legal community rather than the religious community, very little reference will be given to the worship side of Islamic law. In the end, however, it is important to keep in mind that these two duties encompass the whole duty of man, which is the *Shari'a* and the believed pathway to salvation for followers of Islam.

2. Sources of Islamic law and their development

Essentially, there are four established and accepted sources of Islamic law. They are the *Qur'an*, the *Sunnah* of the Prophet Muhammad, Consensus, and Analogical Reasoning. The first two are primary sources of law and are considered to be divine. The final two sources are not considered to be divine because they are tainted by human error. Nevertheless, they are based on the divine sources of law and they are only used when absolutely necessary for reaching a legal conclusion. Additionally, different interpretations of Islamic law recognize certain other secondary sources of law where the primary sources are silent. However, these additional secondary sources of law are not universally recognized in the way that Consensus and Analogical Reasoning are recognized.

a. *The* Qur'an

First, the *Qur'an* is the absolute primary source of law under the *Shari'a* and its text is dispositive on all matters that it addresses. The reason for this is that Muslims believe that it is the direct word of God to mankind with absolutely no taint of human error. The text of the *Qur'an* comprises 114 chapters of 6,236 verses. This text is believed to have been revealed to Muhammad through the intermediary of the angel Gabriel over a period of 22 years. Throughout Muhammad's life, his companions and followers would memorize and recite the text of the *Qur'an*. Further, the literate persons amongst this group would record and preserve portions of the text. It was not until the first Caliphate under Abu Bakr that the whole of the *Qur'an* was compiled into book form. Historicists and scholars, both Muslim and non-Muslim, agree that the book is the greatest piece of classical Arabic literature available.

As aforementioned, Islamic law is a global concept that encompasses the whole duty of man. In the same way, the *Qur'an* is a global text that asserts legal maxims as well as religious truths. As such, scholars generally divide the *Qur'an* into two portions, the Medinan Chapters and the Meccan Chapters (referring to the geographical location of the revelation of the text). The Medinan Chapters provide instructions relating to law, justice, and order, including familial relations, contractual rules, and punishment for crime. The Meccan Chapters largely provide guidance on the religious elements of Islam, including the existence of divine truths, correct religious practices, and defenses of Islam against arguments made by non-believers. As aforementioned, the Meccan Chapters comprise the majority of the *Qur'an*, whereas the "legal" (in the secular sense) contents contained in the Medinan Chapters comprise the minority.

While the *Qur'an* is the ultimate, dispositive source of law in the *Shari'a*, its finite text that was revealed some 1,400 years ago cannot possibly answer directly every legal question that arises after its revelation and recording. No, any reasonably workable and lasting legal system requires flexibility in order to stay in pace with modernity. Thus, Islamic law recognizes the *Sunnah* of the Prophet Muhammad as an alternative source of law to the *Qur'an*.

b. *The* Sunnah

When believers are given a book that is considered to be the direct word of God, they will expectedly conform their lives to its text. By definition, however, a book, is a finite object. It has a defined amount of pages with a certain amount of space available for text. Further, there will likely never be another "edition" of a book like the *Qur'an* because Muslims almost universally agree that it is God's final message to humanity brought by God's final messenger.

Because of the limited nature of the *Qur'an*, coupled with the fact that the law abhors a vacuum, another source of law is necessary to provide guidance on unanswered issues. For this reason, the second source of law – subordinate only to the *Qur'an* – is the *Sunnah* of the Prophet Muhammad.

The word "*sunnah*" literally means "a way for others to follow." The *Sunnah* of the Prophet Muhammad is an extremely broad concept. First, it is necessary to realize that followers of Islam consider Muhammad to be the most important prophet of all time. As such, he is considered to be the most blessed human and, though still but a man, the most rightly guided human that ever did or will walk the earth. Thus, anything that Muhammad ever said or did during his life is extremely likely to be a holy and correct command or action. For this reason, Muslims look to the habits and teachings of Muhammad as an alternate source of law where the *Qur'an* is silent.

The *Sunnah* can essentially be divided into two portions. The first portion comprises the known actions, utterances, and tacit approvals expressed by Muhammad during his life and recorded in a reliable manner. These recordings are collected in *ahadith*. The second portion comprises all of the unknown actions, utterances, and tacit approvals of Muhammad during his life. Unfortunately, the only reliable source of law that can be derived from the *Sunnah* are the *ahadith*, as the unknown portions of the *Sunnah* are lost forever.

Originally, there was no guaranteed way of knowing that any given text proclaimed to be a reliable record of the *Sunnah* was authentic. Even to this day, there is no uniform agreement on what qualifies as an authentic *hadith*. Nevertheless, Islamic scholars engaged in a very important authentication movement over a period of around 300 years that led to the verification of about one million authentic narrations of the actions, utterances, and tacit approvals of Muhammad which are now contained in 4,400 *ahadith*.

When an answer to a legal question cannot be found in the *Qur'an*, Islamic legal practitioners and judges next consult the *ahadith* to determine if the solution was addressed by Muhammad during his life. However, while the *Sunnah* expands the sources of law by adding an extra layer of reliable precedent on top of the *Qur'an*, it is still a finite source of law. That is, Muhammad lived a mortal life and died just as every other mortal does. Much like the *Qur'an*, all of the actions, utterances, and tacit approvals expressed by him during his life can only fill a certain amount of pages and volumes. Further to this point, from a non-religious perspective, Muhammad lived and the *Qur'an* was revealed over 1,400 years ago. How could such relics possibly be able to provide legitimate, workable answers to the pressing moral and legal dilemmas of the 21st century and into the future? For example, are organ transplants, enforcement of intellectual property rights, in vitro fertilization, and withholding life-sustaining medical treatment *Shari'a*-compliant activities? These issues were nonexistent during the life of Muhammad; thus, alternative sources of law are required to provide answers to very important questions like these where the primary sources of law are silent.

c. Ijma

Consensus (*Ijma* in Arabic) is a secondary source of law that, while tainted by human error, is a reliable way to reach correct legal conclusions where the primary sources are silent. One *hadith* narrates Muhammad as saying, "[m]y community will not agree upon error."[2] As such, where the primary sources of law are silent on an issue, agreement of the Muslim community as to the resolution of the issue is sufficient. It is important to note that consensus means unanimous

---

[2] *Sunan* Ibn Majah, 2:1303.

agreement, not majority rule. If even one member dissents, the proposed law is non-binding.

The Muslim community currently consists of over one billion people. Unanimous agreement on even the most basic tenets of Islam is destined to be met with some dissent. For this reason, it is generally understood that the application of *Ijma* requires only the participation of the most respected Islamic scholars of the Muslim community. Nonetheless, their unanimous agreement is required.

Laws created by the consensus of the companions of Muhammad and the earliest Imams of the Islamic society when the Islamic State was intact are generally recognized as valid. Today, however, creating law by consensus is a dubious process due to the fragmentation and severe sectarianism within the global Muslim community. Given this problem, many Islamic law jurisdictions have incorporated religious bodies into the governmental system to create, review, and / or recommend legislation in a quasi-*Ijma* fashion.

d. Qiyas

Analogical reasoning (*Qiyas* in Arabic) is the final established secondary source of law. It is different from *Ijma* in that law created through *Ijma* occurs at the highest echelon of the Islamic society on rare occasions. On the other hand, *Qiyas* occurs at a lower level of society on a daily basis and is only binding on a case by case basis. *Qiyas* is a common method of decision-making in the courts as well as in daily affairs. Specifically, it is the act of taking a recognized and established ruling on one set of facts and applying the same logical rule to another, similar set of facts.

Analogical reasoning can be compared to the use of precedent and the doctrine of *stare decisis*[3] to reach a legal conclusion. However, secular legal systems apply these principles based on earlier decisions made by other courts of law. On the contrary, *Qiyas* under Islamic law is not based on previous rulings made by earthly establishments. Put differently, a valid use of analogical reasoning will only occur by understanding a ruling explicitly laid out in either the *Qur'an* or *Sunnah* and extending that ruling to a similar set of facts. *Qiyas* is not based on the legal reasoning of courts and judges. For this reason, many if not all jurisdictions that apply Islamic law do not recognize the doctrine of *stare decisis* that is recognized in the common law.

An example of an acceptable legal rule derived from *Qiyas* can be seen in the prohibition of pornography in Islam, which is not specifically mentioned in the primary sources of law. However, the *Qur'an* states,

> [t]ell the believing men to reduce [some] of their vision and guard their private parts. That is purer for them. Indeed, Allah is acquainted with what they do. And tell the believing women to reduce [some] of their vision and guard their private parts and not expose their adornment except that which [necessarily] appears thereof and to wrap [a portion of] their headcovers over their chests and not expose their adornment.[4]

This passage admonishes men and women to be modest in the manner of their dress and to resist causing carnal temptation and embracing lust of the flesh. Thus, it can be inferred that producing, distributing, or viewing

---

[3] *Stare decisis* is a doctrine that encourages adherence to legal interpretations and principles laid down in previous judicial rulings. The phrase literally means "to stand by things decided" in Latin.
[4] *Qur'an* 24:30-31.

pornography is analogically forbidden in Islam because of its immodesty and purpose in creating sexual desire.

e. Questionable secondary sources

In addition to the aforementioned sources of law which are universally recognized and largely implemented in Islamic law, there are also certain legal doctrines that are categorized as secondary sources of law which are disputed amongst Islamic scholars today. Due in part to the Islamic community's current state of disarray and sectarian divisiveness (*see infra* Chapter Seven), there is no universal agreement as to the permissibility of these doctrines / secondary sources. Despite the uncertainty and complexity of this reality, it is important to understand the following questionable legal doctrines / secondary sources of law which are applied intermittently in different Islamic law jurisdictions.

i. Ijtihad

The root word for *Ijtihad* is *jihad*, which means "to strive" or "to struggle." Specifically, *Ijtihad* means to strive for a correct legal conclusion through individual reasoning when all other sources of law are silent on the issue. However, any legal ruling derived from the use of *Ijtihad* must have some basis in an established source of law. Essentially, *Ijtihad* is similar to *Qiyas* except that rulings derived from *Ijtihad* become binding on the whole of the Muslim community, while rulings derived from *Qiyas* are only binding on a case by case basis.

The use of *Ijtihad* to reach legal conclusions was prevalent during Muhammad's lifetime and shortly after his death. Later, however, many scholars began to reject the use of *Ijtihad* because they believed that all legal questions had been sufficiently answered by way of the established sources of law. Further, they believed that the use of *Ijtihad* allows for the possibility of corrupting the Islamic religion. Today, the use of *Ijtihad* as a legal source is extremely controversial among Islamic scholars.

ii. *Maslahah Mursalah*

The public interest (*Maslahah Mursalah* in Arabic) may also be considered as a source of law where the primary sources and the recognized secondary sources of law are silent. Essentially, *Maslahah Mursalah* allows for the consideration of the public benefit as a guide for rulemaking and adjudicating disputes. For example, the use of interest in financial transactions is prohibited as a general matter in Islamic law. However, if accepting an interest-based loan from an international organization – such as the International Monetary Fund, for example – benefits the public interest of a struggling Islamic jurisdiction, then the government may perhaps accept the otherwise forbidden loan as a necessity for the public interest.

iii. *Istihsan*

Juristic preference (*Istihsan* in Arabic) refers to the ability of a judge to exercise his personal opinion in rulemaking in a way that works to avoid an unfair outcome that would result from a rigid, literal application of the law. This is similar to the doctrine of equity found in the common law. The use of *Istihsan* could theoretically allow for a judicial ruling that technically goes against the established sources of Islamic law. Hence, *Istihsan* is a very questionable doctrine today.

iv. *'Urf*

Custom (*'Urf* in Arabic) refers to the established practices of a community of reasonable persons. Thus, despite having no basis in the primary sources of law, the customs of a community may be adopted as law, thereby becoming binding upon the entire community. The application of *'Urf* bears similarities to the concept of *jus cogens* in international law. *Jus cogens* norms are created under international law when a significant number of civilized nations consistently recognize a certain, fundamental principle by treating it as a de facto law. When the principle attains the status of a *jus cogens* norm, it becomes binding law upon all nations. For example, the prohibition of slavery is recognized as a *jus cogens* norm in international law due in part to the passage of time and the general acknowledgment of certain human rights recognized by the international community. In the same way, the practice of slavery is largely prohibited in Islamic jurisdictions, despite its permissibility in other sources of law.

3. Divisions in Islamic jurisprudence (*fiqh*)

To begin, the majority of Muslims adhering to the religion of Islam can be divided into two main sects, the largest of which is the *Sunni* sect and the smaller of which is the *Shi'ite* sect. Between 80 to 90 percent of all Muslims in the world follow *Sunni* Islam, while 10 to 20 percent follow *Shi'a* Islam.

A very basic study of the beliefs that separate the *Sunni* sect from the *Shi'ite* sect could very well fill several volumes. In an unjustly general sense, however, the basic reason for the divergent sects comes down to different beliefs regarding the rightful successor of Muhammad. That is, when Muhammad died, his companions and followers had to decide on a successor to be the leader of the Muslim community. The *Sunni* sect believed that Abu Bakr was the most competent and qualified companion for the job, even though he was not related to Muhammad. However, the *Shi'ite* sect believed that leadership of the Muslim community should stay in the bloodline of Muhammad. They believed that Ali ibn Abu Talib, Muhammad's cousin and son-in-law, was the rightful successor. Table 1-1 specifies the geographical influence of both of the main Islamic sects that has prevailed today within the membership of the Organisation of Islamic Cooperation, which is "the collective voice of the Muslim world."[5]

On the whole, there is very little difference between the *Sunni* and *Shi'ite* sects in regard to the transactional duties under the *Shari'a* and most disagreements between the two belief systems are theological in nature only. However, it is important to note that, in addition to this main bifurcation, there are many theological and cultural subdivisions and differences of religious interpretation within these two main sects. For example, there are some extremely conservative branches that occupy a minority following within *Sunni* Islam influenced by such movements as Salifism, which largely calls for a return to the ways and practices of the early Islamic community in all respects. In the same way, *Shi'a* Islam contains its own distinct movements and influences.

In addition to subdivisions in the two main sects of Islam that differ on theological and cultural matters, there are also different schools of legal thought (*fuqaha*) within each sect. For example, there exist four main schools of Islamic jurisprudence under the larger, *Sunni* sect of Islam. They are the schools of opinion, which are comprised of the *Hanafi* and *Shafi'i* schools, and the schools of tradition, which are comprised of the *Hanbali* and *Maliki* schools. Further, *Shi'a* Islam contains its own distinct schools of jurisprudence. All schools of legal thought within Islam recognize the *Qur'an* and *Sunnah* as the paramount sources of law. However, each *fiqh* differs as to the application of established secondary sources of law – including *Ijma* and *Qiyas* – as well as the use of disputed sources – including *Ijtihad, Maslahah Mursalah, Istihsan,* and *'Urf.* Notwithstanding the existence of significant divisions and fragmentations within Islam today, the following Chapters present a basic overview of the whole of Islamic law as recognized by all Muslims, with occasional

---

[5] *See* ORGANISATION OF ISLAMIC COOPERATION, www.oic-oci.org.

references to distinctions maintained by different legal influences.

CHAPTER 2. CONTRACT LAW

A. INTRODUCTION

The humble contract is arguably the most important building block of society. Without it, there can be no functional economy, no productive use of time and resources, and, thus, no legitimate governmental organ to dispense with justice in a fair and equitable manner.

At the outset, it is important to understand the significance of commerce in Islam. On a practical level, the industrious use of one's time and efforts creates social stability and distracts one from evil. In general, more time spent working means less time spent engaging in sinful activities. Further to this point, the Prophet Muhammad (PBUH) was a businessman. In his early years, he would travel with caravans and, later, he would marry Khadyja, a very wealthy widow. Given this information, freedom of contract is found as an overarching theme of Islamic law. Indeed, Islamic legal practitioners will often state "the contract is the *Shari'a* of the parties."

On the whole, the contract law of most jurisdictions does not differ greatly. Indeed, most common and civil law systems generally require the same basic elements in order to form an enforceable agreement. Notwithstanding some peculiar religious factors, Islamic law largely requires the same elements in a contract as do most secular jurisdictions. These basic contractual elements consist of an offer, acceptance of the offer, consideration for the agreement, mutual assent to the deal, and contractual capacity. Further, Islamic law sets out limits on a harmed party's ability to seek damages and remedies from a breaching party for her failure to perform under the contract.

B. OFFER

In general terms, an offer is a proposal to perform an act made to another for the purpose of receiving acceptance of the proposal and, thus, enter into a contractual relationship. The offer is the threshold requirement for all contracts. There can be no acceptance, assent, or valid agreement without first expressing an offer to contract. If an offer is valid, it creates the power of acceptance in the offeree, which gives the offeree the ability to bind the offeror to her promise.

The *Shari'a* is a legal system that encourages commerce and trade. It seeks to reward labor with just compensation and it upholds freedom of contract within religious boundaries. For these reasons, the rules for making a valid offer are liberal. Offers can be expressed orally, in writing, or can be implied in fact by conduct.

1. Oral offer

Oral offers are not necessarily oral. For example, the *Shari'a* recognizes the use of purposeful body language as an effective means of conveying an offer. For offerors who are mute or do not speak the same language as the offeree, offers can be conveyed using handsigns and purposeful body movement.

Notwithstanding the broad scope of oral offers, the validity of an oral offer is limited not by time, but by space. This is referred to as the *majlis* (in Arabic, *majlis* means meeting) rule. In traditional practice (before the advent of telephones, Internet, and the like), merchants, consumers, and all other market participants usually engaged in face to face interaction when negotiating contracts. Islamic law evolved in such a way to conform to this tradition by adopting the *majlis* rule, which holds that an oral offer expires upon the physical separation of the offeror and offeree. Until such physical separation occurs, any oral offer expressed is open to acceptance by the offeree. If the parties separate without concluding the deal, the oral offer expires and any acceptance expressed by the offeree will be invalid.

The *majlis* rule is a default rule. That is, an offeror can orally state the period during which the oral offer is valid and override the application of the *majlis* rule on the expiration of the offer. However, if she neglects to give such a deadline during a face to face negotiation, the *majlis* rule will apply and the oral offer will terminate upon her physical separation from the offeree.

Given the rise of telecommunications and the ability to send instant messages, call, and even have face to face meetings with someone on the opposite side of the planet, it would seem that the *majlis* rule needs to be updated. For example, if two parties engage in negotiations via a videoconference, does an oral offer expressed during the meeting expire after one party signs out of the meeting? Or when she shuts down her computer? Or when she gets up from the computer and leaves the room? The logical extension of the *majlis* rule could apply to any of these contentions. Perhaps the easiest answer is that the offer should expire when the offeror can no longer receive an acceptance of her offer when, for example, either or both of the parties sign off. But in such a case, how would the law handle a sudden, unintended interruption of the Internet connection? As of yet, updating this rule has not been of significant concern to scholars.

Oral offers can also be expressed by a messenger. The person who fills the role of messenger must be a generally trustworthy and upright person in order to ensure that the oral offer expressed by her matches the intent of the real offeror. The *majlis* rule applies to the messenger in the same way that it applies to the offeror; the physical separation of the messenger and the offeree nullifies the offer.

2. Written offer

A writing is sufficient to express an offer, as well. The rules governing written offers are unexceptional. First, a written offer can be made in a meeting, transmitted through the mail, or conveyed via a messenger or agent. When a messenger is used, she must be trustworthy. Initially, the *majlis* rule applied to messengers carrying written offers on behalf of an offeror. That is, the written offer would expire upon the physical separation of the offeree and the messenger. While this may have been feasible in the past, the rule no longer applies to messengers today. Time is money and most messengers, government postal workers for example, are generally not willing to wait while parties peruse offer terms.

After receiving a written offer, the offeree must reply with an acceptance, counteroffer, or denial within a reasonable time. Most scholars agree that the offeree must act quickly to accept a mailed offer, as it will expire after a reasonable time. Notwithstanding this rule, parties can always tailor their offers as they please. For example, an expiration clause setting out the time that a written offer will remain open is a valid condition. Finally, should the offeree fail to respond to a written offer, her silence will probably not suffice as acceptance of the offer (*see infra*).

3. Implied in fact offer

An offer can be implied in fact without using any words, oral or written. For example, some *fuqaha* hold that delivering goods to an individual constitutes an offer to contract. Receiving and using the goods can entail acceptance of the offer and a duty to pay for the goods. However, the offer terms must be explicitly set out with the delivery. For example, the delivery must include some indication of the price expected as payment for the goods.

4. Note on offer terms

The offeror is the master of her offer. As such, the offeror can frame her offer with any conditions that she desires. For example and as aforementioned, the offeror can specify an expiration date for the offer whereby the offer becomes void thereafter. Also, the offeror, for example, can require that the offeree express her acceptance in a certain form, such as orally, in writing, by mail, or otherwise. Failure to adhere to the offeror's conditions on acceptance will usually render the acceptance invalid and the contract voidable at the offeror's discretion.

C. ACCEPTANCE

The power of acceptance is indeed a compelling ability. It gives the offeree the right to bind the offeror to her promise such that her failure to execute the contract gives the offeree a legal claim for money damages or to compel her performance under the contract. However, this power is not without limits. For example, a valid acceptance must match exactly the terms of the offer in order to create a binding contract. Nevertheless, the rules for expressing acceptance of an offer are not much different than the rules for expressing the offer. The acceptance can be oral, written, or implied in fact.

1. Oral acceptance

Notwithstanding any conditions on acceptance stated by the offeror, an oral acceptance is effective under Islamic law to create a binding contract without regard to the form of the offer. That is, an oral acceptance is sufficient to accept a written, implied in fact, or oral offer. In any of these cases, however, the acceptance must be conveyed to the offeror such that she knows her offer has become binding on her.

Like the oral offer, an oral acceptance does not necessarily have to be spoken. Purposeful body movement that indicates an understanding of the terms of the offer and a willingness to conclude the deal is adequate. For example, a simple nodding of the head could suffice.

While purposeful body movement can be a valid expression of acceptance, silence and complete inaction is probably not a sufficient form of acceptance. In most common law jurisdictions, silence can suffice as acceptance when the offer terms specifically state that the offeree's silence is valid to express acceptance and the offeree stays silent with the intent to accept the offer or, alternatively, when the context of the parties' relationship or the market practice shows that silence is a usual and recognized form of acceptance.[6] Because of the *Shari'a*'s prohibitions on uncertainty and gambling, total silence and inaction would probably not suffice as a valid form of acceptance. Some form of indicative conduct, whether oral, written, or otherwise, is required.

An oral acceptance can also be conveyed by a trusted messenger. In such a case, all of the aforementioned rules that apply to the offeree also apply to the messenger who is acting on behalf of the offeree.

2. Written acceptance

Like the oral acceptance, a written acceptance is sufficient to accept any kind of offer (subject to any conditions

---

[6] *See, e.g.*, RESTATEMENT (SECOND) OF CONTRACTS § 69 (1981). *See also* R.L. Ammons v. Wilson & Co. 176 Miss. 645 (Mo. 1936) (finding that a seller's silence could suffice as acceptance of a buyer's offer to purchase shortening where the parties' previous dealings were such that the seller had never expressly accepted the buyer's previous offers but, rather, had consistently fulfilled the buyer's purchase orders within one week of receipt).

contained within the offer), whether oral, implied in fact, or written. A written acceptance can be made in a meeting, conveyed via an agent or trustworthy messenger, or transmitted through the mail.

Acceptance of an offer is effective upon dispatch. In this context, dispatch means placing the writing in the possession of a neutral or "adverse" third party including, for example, the offeror, the offeror's agent, or a postal employee. When the offeree conveys her written acceptance of the offer through the use of the mail, the common law mailbox rule applies under the *Shari'a*. That is, the acceptance is effective upon placing the writing into a mailbox or in the possession of a postal worker. Thus, for example, if the offeree mails her acceptance to the offeror, immediately upon placing the writing in the mail, the contract is in force and the rights and duties thereunder become binding on both parties.

3. Implied in fact acceptance

While complete silence and inaction is probably not a sufficient form of acceptance under Islamic law, acceptance of an offer can be implied in fact by the offeree's conduct, regardless of whether the offer was oral, written, or itself implied in fact by the offeror's conduct. The kind of conduct that implies acceptance of an offer is dependent upon the type of contract sought to be concluded. In a contract for goods, taking possession of and using the goods is sufficient conduct to imply that the offeree agrees with the terms of the offer and wishes to enter into a contract, which entails the offeree's payment of consideration for the goods. In a contract for services, the offeree's performance of the service can be sufficient to indicate her acceptance of the offer and willingness to make a contract. After her performance, the offeror will be obliged to pay the consideration specified in her offer.

4. Counteroffer: defective acceptance

As aforementioned, any terms stated in an acceptance must match exactly the terms of the offer. This requirement stems from the prohibitions on engaging in *gharar* (excessive risk / uncertainty, *see infra*) under Islamic law. Thus, any deviation from the terms of the offer is not sufficient to express a valid acceptance that binds the offeror to her offer. Rather, such deviation would be considered a counteroffer that destroys the original offer.

For example, in a contract for the sale of grain, assume that the offeror says to the offeree, "I will give you 10 dirhams for a bushel of grain," the offeree replies, "I accept, but for 15 dirhams," and the offeror declines. In this example, the offeree cannot later seek to accept and / or enforce the offeror's original offer of 10 dirhams for a bushel of grain. Any deviation in the terms of the original offer expressed by the offeree destroys the original offer expressed by the offeror and acts as a counteroffer. Of course, the offeror is free to restate her original offer.

When an offeree expresses a defective acceptance in the form of a counteroffer, the offeree and the original offeror switch places. That is, the offeree becomes the offeror, the offeror becomes the offeree, and the contractual formation process begins anew.

D. Consideration

Even if parties have expressed a willingness to enter into a contractual relationship by communicating an offer and acceptance of the offer with mutual assent to conclude the deal, consideration for the contract is required in order to enforce it. To begin, it is important to particularly define the concept of consideration under the *Shari'a*. In general terms, consideration can be any object that has value, a legal right or forbearance of a legal right, service, or an otherwise tangible or intangible object that is bargained for in exchange for another valuable object, legal right or forbearance of a legal right, service, or otherwise tangible or intangible object. The concept of consideration for a contract found in the common law is not significantly different than that of the *Shari'a*. However, there are a few peculiar differences herein discussed. The consideration for a contract must be specifically defined, possible to perform, valuable, and lawful under the *Shari'a*.

1. Specificity

First, the consideration for a contract must be fully known by both parties. That is, all important features of the consideration must be particularly described such that no party will be surprised when the other party performs. Islamic law forbids contractual and commercial relations involving *gharar* (excessive risk / uncertainty, *see infra*). It is important to note that a contract concluded without a sufficiently particular description of the consideration entails excessive risk and is unenforceable.

2. Possibility

Second, it must be absolutely possible for the parties to a contract to be able to provide the consideration under Islamic law. That is, the consideration must be existent, owned by the contracting party, and capable of being delivered to the counterparty. For example, a contract where an offeror promises to give her neighbor's automobile to the offeree in exchange for money is unenforceable. Not only does the offeror lack title to the automobile, but she also cannot deliver the vehicle to the offeree free of encumbrances (i.e., the neighbor's ownership).

3. Legality

Next, the consideration for a contract must be a lawful object or purpose under the large umbrella of Islam. This requirement entails not only transactional duties between mankind, but also duties of worship between God and man. For example, any object that entails usury (*riba*), excessive risk or uncertainty (*gharar*), alcohol, pork, or any other forbidden characteristic under the *Shari'a* is insufficient consideration.

4. Value

Next, anything offered as consideration for a contract must have value under Islamic law. As discussed more fully later, a contract for a peppercorn in exchange for a mansion is likely unenforceable under the *Shari'a*. Further, Islamic law holds that some objects are worthless and are, thus, insufficient as consideration. For example, a contract for pork or alcohol is unenforceable for many reasons, one of which is that these objects generally hold no value under Islamic law.

5. Proportionality of consideration

Finally, an important principle of Islamic contract law is the concept that objects, both tangible and intangible, should be exchanged for equally valuable objects and, further, that labor should be rewarded with its full and just value. Islamic law holds that disproportionate consideration under a contract is a form of unjust enrichment to one party that results in an injustice to the other party, which is considered a form of usury (*riba*).

a. Historical framework

A hallmark of Western legal systems is an almost immutable respect for freedom of contract. For example, the exchange of a peppercorn for a multimillion dollar mansion is not necessarily a void transaction that is immediately unenforceable in all Western jurisdictions. Indeed, many common law jurisdictions would enforce such a contract on the grounds that parties should "act like adults" in their transactions and that the courts are not meant to be "nannies" that constantly undo the poor choices of unthinking and / or unfortunate contracting parties. That is, assuming that all other contractual requirements are met, the parties are free to make their own choices as they please.

Under a theory of Islamic law, however, this type of transaction is troublesome because, even if all other contractual elements are met, a transaction wherein one party offers something of minimal value in exchange for something of significant value seems to entail unjust enrichment. Indeed, one party might agree to a disproportionate contract with the hope that doing so might lead to some unspoken, unwritten future benefit with the other party, such as receiving a good deal in future contracts, receiving a recommendation for a job, or being allowed to marry his daughter. Then, if the hoped for future benefit does not occur, the party that accepted the bad deal might harbor bitterness and anger towards the counterparty.

From a religious and historical standpoint, this was a serious problem in the nascency of Islam and throughout Muhammad's life. That is, the Muslim community was quite small and very much outnumbered by the other religious groups in the Arabian Gulf. In order to achieve solidarity and strength to be able to survive as an oppressed and persecuted group, the early Muslim community had to adopt commercial rules that sought, above all, to foster fairness and equity between each other, perhaps to the detriment of economic growth.[7]

---

[7] See TIMUR KURAN, THE LONG DIVERGENCE: HOW ISLAMIC LAW HELD BACK THE MIDDLE EAST (Princeton University Press 2011) for a clear and thorough analysis of this concept. Kuran compares the Islamic law of contract, liability, and business associations with that of Europe

The historical reasons for this strict rule requiring proportionality of consideration have perpetuated the rule up to the present day. However, from an evidentiary standpoint, it is easier to determine whether the values of the considerations to a contract are proportionate than it is to determine whether one party was intoxicated, joking, or otherwise insincere when concluding an outrageous contract. For this reason, Islamic law not only requires equal consideration for contracts, but all of the terms of the contract and the specifications of the consideration must be particularly described in sufficient detail.

b. Gift contracts

While equality of consideration is required under Islamic law, gratuitous promises are also enforceable. A gift contract is a statement from a promisor to a promisee wherein the promisor states that he will give some consideration to the promisee as a gift expecting nothing in return. At first glance, this seems like an unenforceable contract under the *Shari'a* because, not only is the promisor not receiving an item of

---

during the reign of the Ottoman Empire. Further, Kuran analyzes several cases brought before the Ottoman courts involving the commercial disputes of both European foreigners and Ottoman subjects. In these cases, the Ottoman courts generally applied European law to European disputes and Islamic law to disputes between Ottoman subjects. Kuran argues that the prevailing European commercial law was superior to Islamic commercial law because it struck a perfect balance between risk and reward while providing for the possibility of long-term business practices. Due to these factors, Kuran argues, Europe flourished while the Ottoman Empire and Islamic jurisdictions languished. Indeed, Kuran's arguments are compelling as the effects of the disparities between European and Islamic commercial norms can arguably be observed today. That is, European cultural, economic, religious, legal, and other influences are widespread, while Islamic influences are isolated and sometimes considered archaic. In addition, Western European influenced systems enjoy economic dominance in the world today while the Middle East and Islamic influenced countries are largely still in a developing state.

minimal value in return for her consideration, but she is receiving absolutely nothing at all for it.

However, Islam encourages and rewards the giving of gifts, forgiving of debts, and otherwise charitable acts performed by believers. An act of selfless charity is considered to be immediately rewarded with God's favor and blessings and is, thus, exchanged with an equally valuable consideration. Therefore, in theory, a promise to give a gift is an enforceable promise.

E. MUTUAL ASSENT

Islamic contract law strongly prohibits the existence of uncertainty and excessive risk (*gharar*) in contractual relations. As such, the mutual assent of all parties to enter into a contractual relationship is an essential element for a valid contract. Mutual assent to enter into a contractual relationship whereby both parties are bound to perform under the agreement is achieved by adhering to the aforementioned rules requiring specificity in the terms of the offer, acceptance, and in the description of the consideration. When specificity is lacking such that the parties have different expectations under the contract, then the agreement is voidable for lack of mutual assent.

F. CAPACITY

All parties must have the capacity to enter into a contractual relationship in order to form a valid contract. Incapacitation can occur as a result of a party's physical state, mental condition, and / or financial situation. Any defect in a party's capacity to contract renders the contract voidable by the incapacitated party, even if all other elements of the contract are sufficient.

1. Physical state

Islamic law looks to the physical state of contracting parties as part of the analysis required to determine if a party has contractual capacity. Capacity is inferred by the party's physical maturity as well as her physical health.

a. *Physical maturity*

Most common law and civil law jurisdictions have statutes that specifically designate when a person has contractual capacity based on age. For example, many U.S. states hold that parties have capacity to contract on the day before they reach the age of 18 years. At the same time, many jurisdictions that are influenced in whole or in part by Islamic law also have a basic statutory framework that prescribes, among other things, the age whereupon a party gains contractual capacity. For example, the countries Qatar, Bahrain, Jordan, and Syria, while heavily influenced by Islamic law, specify 18 years as the age of contractual capacity.

Perhaps a statutory designation of the age of contractual capacity is easy to implement and offers a rare circumstance where a bright-line rule in the law makes sense. However, Islamic law is more flexible and looks, among other things, not to a contracting party's age, but to her physical maturity as a factor in her contractual capacity. Under a non-statutory strictly *Shari'a* framework, post-pubescent sexual maturity is required in order for a party to have contractual capacity. In this regard, Islamic law infers mental maturity and commercial reliability from physical maturity.

However, incapacitated minors can still conclude contracts by way of a guardian. In this regard, the guardian acts somewhat as an agent on behalf of the minor party and can bind the minor to perform under the contract. However, a guardian has the authority to act on behalf of a minor even if doing so is against the minor's wishes. Nevertheless, guardians have a duty to act in the best interests of the minor parties for whom they act at all times. Generally, a father acts as guardian over his minor children. However, if the father is unable or unwilling to act as guardian, the role can be filled by an older male relative, including grandfathers, uncles, and older brothers. The ability to act as guardian over a male minor is terminated at puberty. Alternatively, a qualifying male relative's guardianship over a female continues until the woman is married, at which point guardianship transfers to her husband.

b. Physical health

Next, a party with a physically debilitating terminal illness lacks contractual capacity. It is important to note that this element of capacity is a two part inquiry: 1) the illness must be physically debilitating; and 2) the illness must be a terminal illness. For the first inquiry, the physical nature, not the mental nature, of the illness is what matters. That is, a party can be fully knowledgeable, competent, and coherent but still lack contractual capacity if she is inflicted with a terminal illness that severely restricts her ambulatory abilities and / or causes intense pain. Second, a terminal illness is one that is incurable and reasonably likely to lead to an early death.

2. Mental condition

In order to have contractual capacity, the parties must desire to and be seriously intent on entering into a contractual relationship, while understanding fully their rights and obligations under the contract. Parties lack the requisite mental capacity to contract when a contract is made while either or both parties are joking, under duress, insane, or intoxicated.

a. Joking

There is no legal formula for determining when the terms of a party's offer or acceptance to enter into a contract are expressed in jest. However, when it is evident that a party is jokingly expressing words or conduct that would otherwise constitute a serious desire to create a contract, the joking party is considered to lack the requisite mental condition for contractual capacity.

b. Duress

Another instance where a party is deemed to lack contractual capacity is when she enters the contract knowingly, but does so under duress. A party enters into a contract under duress when she lacks the free will to consent to the deal.

Islamic law applies a three-part subjective inquiry to determine when a contracting party is under duress such that she lacks contractual capacity: 1) there must be a threat by one party to another party to induce agreement to a contract (the threatening party does not necessarily have to be the counterparty in the contract); 2) the threatened party must have a subjectively authentic fear of the threat; and 3) the threatening party must be capable of effecting the threat.

c. Insanity

Mental sanity is required for a party to have contractual capacity. Mental insanity negates contractual capacity and occurs when a party fails to understand the consequences of her conduct because of a mental impediment. This can occur as a result of mental incoherence caused by a permanent or long-lasting mental disease that renders a party incompetent for life or an otherwise lengthy duration of time.

d. Intoxication

Finally, a party lacks the requisite mental condition to conclude a contract when the party is intoxicated. Intoxication can occur by ingesting substances that are forbidden under Islamic law, such as alcohol or illicit drugs. However, ingesting an approved mind-altering substance that is necessary for some medical or other legitimate purpose can also result in intoxication. For example, ingesting prescription pain medications that cause severe drowsiness may render a contracting party incapacitated. In any case, intoxication negates contractual capacity.

3. Financial situation

In addition to a party's physical and mental condition, contractual capacity is determined by a party's financial state. A demonstrated character of recklessness in financial dealings as well as insolvency are sufficient features to negate a party's contractual capacity.

a. Recklessness

When a party has repeatedly shown herself to be wasteful and extravagant, the party is deemed to lack contractual capacity. Even if the reckless party is capable of concluding the deal and understands her rights and obligations under the contract, she is still considered incapacitated under Islamic law. Of course, after a reasonable amount of time wherein the reckless party proves herself to be financially responsible in the community, she will be deemed to have regained her capacity to contract.

b. Insolvency

Next, a financially insolvent party lacks contractual capacity. That is, a person who lacks the ability to pay her bills also lacks the ability to contract. It is important to note the distinction between insolvency and financial recklessness.

First, an insolvent person is one who has little or no money. Insolvency can occur as a result of irresponsible financial dealings, but it can also occur due to other circumstances wholly or partially outside of the control of the insolvent person. For example, a person can be rendered insolvent through no fault of their own due to a natural catastrophe that wipes out her home and / or business. Or, a person can be rendered insolvent due to compelling and insurmountable market pressures. Indeed, many of the most successful and influential businesspeople throughout history have, at one point, experienced insolvency.

On the other hand, a financially reckless person may or may not have money. The only issue is whether the person has demonstrated a character for being reckless and wasteful with her money. If so, then the party lacks contractual capacity, even if she is extremely wealthy.

Obviously, this distinction is troublesome due to the fact that different people with different income brackets enjoy different standards of living. Furthermore, the distinction is even more complicated due to the fact that those in power often influence the law. Indeed, many leaders of Islamic nations would most certainly be deemed financially reckless due to their extravagant expenditures on unnecessary items of luxury. Nevertheless, the rule is laid out in Islamic law and is binding.

G. DAMAGES AND REMEDIES

Finally, it is important to note that Islamic courts have wide discretion to order remedies when a valid contract has been breached. Generally, remedies for breaching a contractual promise under Islamic law include money damages, specific performance, and imprisonment.

1. Money damages

First, when a contracting party has breached a valid contract, an Islamic court can order that the breaching party compensate the harmed party for her loss. In this regard, however, the amount that must be paid in money damages must reflect only the actual damage caused by the breach. That is, Islamic law does not recognize any form of punitive damages, which go beyond the actual damage and are meant to deter future egregious behavior. The reason for this limit to money damages stems from the prohibition of unjust enrichment (*riba*) under the *Shari'a*. That is, it is unjust for one to receive compensation when she has not exerted any effort in return for it.

This requirement carries over even if the contract contained a liquidated damages clause.[8] That is, if the stipulated amount of money to be paid in the event of breach under the liquidated damages clause exceeds the actual damages of the harmed party, then the Islamic court will disregard the clause and award an appropriate amount of money instead.

Notwithstanding this requirement, some contracts that involve payment of funds may contain liquidated damages, as long as the excess of the actual damages is not used to benefit the harmed party. For example, a lease contract may specify a certain amount of money that must be paid as a penalty if the lessee fails to pay rent on time. However, the amount paid as a penalty must reflect only the lessor's actual damages, which are usually just administrative expenses (e.g., sending correspondence to or calling the lessee to remind her that she must pay, legal fees involved with filing court documents against her, etc.). Generally, the lessor will donate

---

[8] A liquidated damages clause sets forth a fixed amount of money in the contract that each party agrees to pay in the event that it breaches the contract.

any amount that exceeds her actual damages to a charitable organization, thus incentivizing the lessee to pay on time, while operating within the contractual prohibitions of Islamic law.

2. Specific performance and imprisonment

Specific performance is a valid contractual remedy under Islamic law. That is, when a party breaches the contract by failing to perform her contractual duties, an Islamic court can order that the breaching party perform the neglected duties as contracted. This includes both contracts involving services, goods, and payment of money. However, when the breaching party's duty under the contract entails payment of a debt, the court can order her imprisonment. But, imprisonment is only valid as a remedy when the breaching party has the ability to pay the debt, yet refuses to do so. Thus, a party that is declared bankrupt cannot be imprisoned for failing to pay contractual debts.

CHAPTER 3. PROPERTY LAW

A. INTRODUCTION

The manner in which a given jurisdiction deals with issues of property ownership speaks volumes about that jurisdiction's culture, historical roots, standard of living, and ability to maintain order and justice. This concept can be seen in the profound differences between most capitalist and communist jurisdictions. For example, a strictly capitalist system highly favors individual property rights and presumes that property should be privately owned. On the other hand, a communist system operates from the other extreme and favors public ownership of property. Under Islamic law, however, the earth and all material objects within it are deemed to be the property of God, with mankind acting as trustee over it.

The property jurisprudence found within the sources of Islamic law draw on the historical roots developed during Islam's nascency in the Arabian Gulf. While this jurisprudence can be considered neither strictly capitalist nor strictly communist, Islamic law tends to incorporate portions of both theories. Indeed, many scholars, after examining the property jurisprudence of Islamic law, have called it a "Third Way" that strikes a perfect balance between two extremes.

While each legal system that is influenced by Islam will inevitably apply the principles of Islamic law differently, the overarching historical and religious aspects of the *Shari'a* in regard to property law are quite simple. Islamic law addresses the issues related to acquiring and transferring title as well as necessary restrictions on private ownership of property.

B. THE CONCEPT OF "PROPERTY" UNDER THE *SHARI'A*

Under Islamic law, the whole earth and everything in it is the rightful property of God alone. However, God has placed mankind on the earth as well and allows mankind to possess the earth and everything in it, acting as trustee over it. For this reason, people are permitted to privately own property.

As defined under Islamic law, property is any object that has value, whether tangible or intangible. Value is measured in terms of objective reasonableness (i.e., what would an objectively reasonable person deem valuable?). However, some Islamic schools of thought hold that an object can only be considered as property if it has value in the absence of necessity. For example, pork is an object that is forbidden under the *Shari'a* and, thus, only has value in the urgent scenario of starvation when eating the forbidden meat becomes necessary for survival.

Most legal systems, including the *Shari'a*, divide the concept of property into two subcategories consisting of both real and personal property. Real property consists of land and all physical objects attached thereto, while personal property consists of all moveable objects. However, certain intangible rights and concepts can also be considered as property. For example, Islamic law recognizes easements, usufructs, and spousal consortium as property. Further, intellectual property, which is becoming progressively important with the advent of increased technological advancement, is also recognized as property under the *Shari'a* because it has value.

C. ACQUISITION AND TRANSFER OF TITLE

Having defined the concept of property under Islamic law, it is important to understand the manner in which one acquires title to and transfers title to property. One can acquire title to unowned property by exercising dominion over and deriving a benefit from it. However, title to owned property can be acquired and transferred by way of sale, pledge, adverse possession, and findings.

1. Unowned property

Property without a titleholder is property that brings little benefit to the public interest. As such, the policy of Islamic law seeks to encourage the acquisition of title over unowned property so that the property can be exploited, thereby contributing to the survival and expansion of the community. Essentially, title to both real and personal unowned property vests in a person who exercises dominion over the property with the intent to acquire title thereto.

An individual exercises dominion over unowned property by controlling, occupying, or possessing it, or by exerting efforts to extract a benefit from it. On the other hand, title to unowned property does not vest in one who asserts ownership over it with words alone. For example, placing a label on the property – such as a sign that asserts one's ownership – is insufficient.

Rather, the individual must engage in behavior that is deserving of compensation in the form of title to the property. For example, building a house and living on the unowned property and excluding third parties from entering it would probably be a sufficient form of controlling and occupying the property that would lead to acquisition of title. In the same way, claiming ownership over the property, leasing it to third parties, and excluding unauthorized third parties from entering might also be sufficient. Finally, expending significant time and / or resources to extract a benefit from unowned property is activity that merits compensation in the form of title to the property. For example, tilling a field on unowned land, planting wheat on it, and harvesting the crop would probably be sufficient to give title to the person who worked on the land.

2. Owned property

Title to owned property can be transferred from the titleholder to another person. An individual can acquire title to owned property by sale, pledge, or adverse possession. Further, one can acquire title to lost property in certain circumstances by finding it.

a. Sale

An owner can transfer title to her property by selling it to a buyer. However, the terms of the transfer are subject to the Islamic law of contracts (*see supra* Chapter Two).

b. Pledge

A debtor's title to property can transfer to her creditor in a pledge transaction in certain circumstances. In a pledge transaction, the debtor offers her property as security in exchange for a loan from a creditor. In doing so, the creditor or an authorized third party takes possession of the property and the debtor retains deficient title. During the period of possession, the creditor or authorized third party is liable for any foreseeable damage to the pledged property. Further, the debtor lacks the ability to alienate the pledged property until the loan is repaid in full. When the loan is satisfied, full title to the pledged property reverts to the debtor. However, if the debtor fails to repay the debt, her deficient title to the pledged property is extinguished and transferred to the creditor or an authorized third party.

c. Adverse possession

In common law jurisdictions, adverse possession is a manner in which title to real property is transferred, perhaps unwillingly, from its owner to an adverse possessor. In this circumstance, the adverse possessor must exercise open and notorious, exclusive, and continuous control over the land that is adverse to the rights of the true owner. Further, many jurisdictions require the adverse possessor to maintain such control over the property for a prescribed statutory period, which usually ranges anywhere from ten to thirty years.

The policy behind the theory of adverse possession is similar to the policy in awarding title to an individual that uses or extracts a benefit from unowned land (*see supra*). That is, property should be owned by a competent individual who will use and exploit the property, which thereby contributes to the survival and growth of the community. Under Islamic law, however, purposeful and unlawful possession of another's property without compensation is extremely discouraged.[9] Rather, an individual who believes that a landowner has neglected or failed to properly exploit her land must approach the competent religious or governmental body for permission to seek title to the land.

If the authorities agree with the individual, then they may grant her a period of three years to possess the land and attempt to put it to use. If after three years the individual fails to realize a benefit, then she must vacate the premises immediately unless the authorities grant an extension of time. If, however, she does put the land to a beneficial use, then full title to the land is transferred to her from the true owner.

d. Finders law

The policy behind the law of findings is to reunite lost property with its true owner. If returning lost property to the true owner is not possible, however, the property should be used for the benefit of the public.

A finder of lost property acts as a trustee over it until the true owner of the lost property is found. Once the true owner

---

[9] "Narrated Said bin Zaid: Allah's Apostle said, 'Whoever usurps the land of somebody unjustly, his neck will be encircled with it down the seven earths (on the Day of Resurrection)'" Vol. 3, Book 43, *Hadith* 632.

proves her title over the lost property, the finder must return it to her. Because the finder was a trustee over the property, she remains liable for any damage that may have occurred to the lost property during her possession thereof. The true owner, however, must compensate the finder for any costs or resources that the finder expended in improving the value of the lost property while the finder was trustee over the property. Finally, if the true owner of the lost property is a non-Muslim, she will be taxed at one-fifth of the value of the property upon retaking possession thereof. On the other hand, Muslim owners are not taxed when they retake possession of their lost property.

Contrarily, if a true owner of lost property cannot establish title after a reasonable period of time, then title to the property will pass to a third party. In this situation, there are three possibilities. First, title to lost property passes to the finder if she found the lost property on unowned land. Second, title to lost property passes to the public if the lost property was found on public land. Third, if lost property was found on owned land, then title to the lost property passes to the landowner. However, if the landowner cannot be ascertained or refuses to take title to the property, then title also passes to the public.

Importantly, no matter where lost property was found, the finder is always the trustee over property which she finds until possession is regained by the true owner or title passes to someone else. Thus, for example, if lost property is found on an individual's land and the true owner never establishes her title, the landowner must request that the finder turn over the property. If the finder refuses to turn over the property to the landowner, who holds title to the property, then the landowner may sue the finder for return of the property.

D. RESTRICTIONS ON PRIVATE PROPERTY

Ownership and control over one's private property is a sacrosanct right under Islamic law. Notwithstanding religious identification, however, many influential jurists and scholars have noted that individuals tend to utilize, maintain, and maximize the economic output of property in a more effective and efficient manner than does the state or a governmental body. Even so, all jurisdictions recognize that there are times when the sanctity of private ownership of property must give way to a compelling need of neighbors or the public at large. The *Shari'a* is no different in that private ownership of property is freely permitted within the carefully denoted confines of Islam. Specifically, neighbors and the public have certain rights to use and control another's land as well as the water resources thereon. And, the state may expropriate private property on behalf of the public in certain circumstances, including for *Zakat*.

1. Easements and water law

Under the common law, an easement is a legal right to use or control another's land for a certain purpose. An easement right can be created by express agreement between the landowner and the third party or, alternatively, an easement right can be implied by necessity. For example, where one landowner has no reasonable access to a main roadway, an easement may be implied by necessity that allows the landowner to enter upon and cross her neighbor's land to access the roadway.

Islamic law fully recognizes the concept of easements under the common law. However, the *Shari'a* also recognizes the importance of access to water in considering when entering another's private property should be allowed. Specifically, the presence of a water source on private property can create an easement implied by necessity. That is, travelers have an easement right to enter upon another's private land in order to gain access to a stream or body of water on the individual's land in order to, for example, provide water for camels and livestock. In the same way, private landowners are not permitted to obstruct streams or rivers which originate or cross through their land such that neighbors downstream are deprived of their right to enjoy the free flow of the water.

2. Eminent domain and the public interest

In general, complete and unrestricted ownership over private property is protected and encouraged under Islamic law. Notwithstanding this general rule, in certain extreme circumstances the public interest in an individual's private property may outweigh the private interest in complete and unrestricted ownership of property. When this occurs, the Islamic authority may use its power to expropriate the private property. However, the state must compensate the aggrieved private party for the value of her expropriated property.

The public benefit is served by such institutions and structures as schools, hospitals, roads, mosques, and any other structure deemed necessary to the public interest by the Islamic authority. As such, private property can be expropriated when necessary to construct such structures, as long as the owner is compensated for her loss.

However, the public good and the survival of the Islamic state also depend on the proper use and stewardship over the community's natural resources. In this sense, the Prophet Muhammad (PBUH) said, "Muslims have common share in three things: grass, water and fire."[10] In the context of the early Islamic community and its location in the desert regions of the Arabian Gulf, this *hadith* seems reasonable. Grass, water, and wood are scarce resources in arid and dry

---

[10] *Sunan* Abi Dawud, Book 23, *Hadith* 3470.

conditions. Further, water is a basic element of life, grass is a food source for herds of animals, and wood is necessary to use as fuel to sustain fire for cooking and warmth.

Traditionally, private ownership of land containing natural resources such as freshwater sources, grasslands, and forests was respected under Islamic rule. However, failure to properly conserve such resources can endanger the entire Islamic community and, thus, call for intervention by the state on behalf of the people.

Some contemporary jurists have argued that the modern-day analogs to grass, water, and fire are also susceptible to expropriation in the public interest. For example, oil is a necessary resource for virtually all countries today in a variety of industries, including manufacturing and construction as well as transportation of people and goods. Thus, petroleum reservoirs lying underneath private property may be expropriated for the public interest if they are not properly conserved. However, some scholars have cited to this *hadith* when calling for the outright nationalization of all oil reserves.

Finally, when a person hoards her property for the purpose of artificially inflating its value, the state can step in and seize the private property with compensation in the amount of the true value of the property. Importantly, individuals are permitted to store up their property in preparation for times of want. Further, nothing forbids such individuals from selling property at a higher-than-normal value during times of want. However, it is the act of taking advantage of the community by artificially controlling the market unfairly that authorizes the state to exercise its eminent domain power over private property.

3. *Zakat*

Finally, it is important to note that one of the five pillars of Islam (*see supra* Chapter One) crosses into the transactional sphere of Islamic property law. As aforementioned, *Zakat* in Arabic means "to purify or develop" and is referred to as "charity" or "almsgiving." However, *Zakat* is actually a legal right held by the poor. The purpose of *Zakat* is to correct imbalances in the social structure and provide for the needy. However, the giver of *Zakat* also benefits by assuring for herself rewards in the hereafter.

First, Islamic law holds that a Muslim is only liable for payment of *Zakat* if the amount of her wealth meets a certain threshold. This amount, called *nisab*, has fluctuated throughout Islamic history. However, one *hadith* states that the value of the *nisab* can be measured in terms of livestock. Specifically, the *hadith* sets the value of the *nisab* at five camels, thirty cattle, or forty sheep and goats.[11]

Next, the amount that an individual must pay in *Zakat* is based on all property owned by the individual for one lunar year. However, only the amount of such property that exceeds the value of the *nisab* is taxable. Generally, scholars agree that the *Zakat* is calculated at 2.5 percent of any cash income, 5 to 10 percent of any agricultural income, and 20 percent of any income received by extracting natural resources or minerals from the earth.

Finally, failure to pay the required amount of wealth in *Zakat* can lead to the seizure of property in order to satisfy the unpaid amount. However, the greater punishment for failing to pay *Zakat* as required is not levied on earth, but in the hereafter. That is, paying *Zakat* is one of the five pillars of Islam and is an extremely important aspect of submission to

---

[11] Muwatta Malik, Book 17, *Hadith* 24.

God. Thus, failing to pay *Zakat* severely hampers one's ability to achieve salvation in the hereafter.

CHAPTER 4. BANKING AND FINANCE LAW

A. Introduction

Banking and finance law is not usually considered a foundational topic that is included in an introduction to a jurisdiction's legal system. For an introductory study of the *Shari'a*, however, this topic is of utmost important for both scholarly and practical reasons.

For scholarly purposes, the historical background of Islam and the spirit of Islamic commercial law are encapsulated in the banking and finance jurisprudence of the *Shari'a*. For practical purposes, however, Islamic banking and finance law is an extremely pertinent topic today because it is an industry that is booming. Globally, Islamic banks held about USD 250 billion in assets in 2008, a figure which was predicted to increase by 15 percent per year.[12] Indeed, *Shari'a*-compliant assets worldwide were valued at USD 822 billion in 2010, a 29 percent increase in value from the previous year.[13]

Before embarking on this topic, however, it is important to note that grossly capitalized and highly regulated local, national, and international banks did not exist during the Prophet Muhammad's (PBUH) life over 1,400 years ago. Thus, many of the foregoing rules are not strictly stated in the "black letter law" of the *Qur'an* and *Sunnah*. Rather, the rules have been developed as a result of using the secondary

---

[12] MARTIN CIHAK AND HEIKO HESSE, ISLAMIC BANKS AND FINANCIAL STABILITY: AN EMPIRICAL ANALYSIS 3 (International Monetary Fund 2008).
[13] *Shari'a Calling*, THE ECONOMIST (Nov. 12, 2009), www.economist.com/node/14859353.

sources of law described in Chapter One. These sources of law have helped Islamic scholars to create rules for permissible banking and financing activities that encourage commerce and growth, while preserving the historical and religious framework of the *Shari'a*.

B. ISLAMIC FINANCE

Finance, for purposes of this Chapter, refers to the act of supplying capital to another for the purpose of receiving a higher amount than the supplied capital, creating a return on the investment. Financing inevitably involves some sort of contractual relationship. Thus, it is important to keep in mind the principles of Islamic contract law discussed in Chapter Two. Indeed, Islamic finance is essentially a subcategory of Islamic contract law that is used specifically for investment purposes.

The goal of Islamic finance is to encourage investors to seek the rewards that conventional finance offers while operating within the carefully prescribed religious boundaries of the *Shari'a*. This goal can be achieved by using longstanding *Shari'a*-compliant financial instruments in financial dealings that avoid the aforementioned prohibited elements of usury (*riba*) and excessive risk (*gharar*).

1. Forbidden contractual elements

As noted in Chapter Two, forbidden elements contained within a contract are void under Islamic law. The most pertinent contractual elements that must be avoided in the field of banking and finance law include *riba* (unjust enrichment / interest) and *gharar* (excessive risk). As such, entering into a conventional loan is impermissible because the use of interest is prohibited. Usury (*riba*) has an intriguing and perhaps dubious historical background.

a. Usury (riba)

Under Islamic law, a "loan" is the act of lending any object of value to another with no profit-seeking motive. That is, the exact value of the loaned capital must be returned to the lender, no more. Any excess in value that is returned to a lender in payment for a loan is considered usury (riba) and is forbidden under Islamic law. Thus, for example, a mortgage loan with a three percent interest rate, a credit card with a ten percent interest rate, and a school loan with a six percent interest rate are all prohibited under the Shari'a. In these scenarios, the lender is giving money to the borrower with the expectation that the borrower will pay a greater sum than what was lent over a period of time.

From a historical perspective, Islamic scholars are not absolutely certain about the meaning of riba in the context of the Qur'an and Sunnah, nor are they completely unified in their beliefs on the extent to which interest should be forbidden. In the pre-Islamic Arabian Gulf, it is possible that riba involved the specific practice of doubling a borrower's debt immediately upon default and redoubling the amount on each subsequent day that the debt was not paid. For example, the Qur'an states, "[y]ou who believe, do not consume usurious interest, doubled and redoubled."[14]

However, riba also seems to refer to a wider constraint that requires all commercial exchanges to be equal in value. For example, one hadith reports that,

> [t]he Prophet said, '[t]he selling of wheat for wheat is riba except if it is exchanged from hand to hand and equal in amount. Similarly the selling of barley for barley is riba except if it is from hand to hand and

---

[14] Qur'an 3:130.

71

equal in amount, and dates for dates is *riba* except if it is from hand to hand and equal in amount.'[15]

In any case, the punishment for indebtedness was enslavement. Those who could not pay their debts were forced to work as slaves until the unpaid amount was satisfied. Thus, some commentators argue that the total prohibition on interest that has prevailed into the modern era is wholly incorrect because Muhammad's intent in forbidding *riba* was aimed solely at ending the practice of enslavement for indebtedness, which had grown out of control. Nonetheless, the prohibition on *riba* was the final Quranic revelation conveyed to Muhammad and the exact purpose for prohibiting *riba* was not revealed during his life. One *hadith* reports that "[t]he last thing to be revealed was the [Quranic] Verse on *riba* but the Messenger of Allah died before he had explained it to us."[16]

b. *Excessive risk* (gharar)

One *hadith* notes that "[t]he *gharar* sale includes selling fish that are in the water, selling a slave that has escaped, selling birds that are in the sky, and similar types of sales."[17] In the same way, uncertainty, gambling, and excessive risk are all forbidden practices under the *Shari'a*. The main purpose for these constraints lies in the ideals of fairness and communal harmony sought to be achieved by the principles of Islam. For example, the *Qur'an* states, "Satan only wants to cause between you animosity and hatred through intoxicants and gambling [i.e., excessive risk] and to avert you from the remembrance of Allah and from prayer. So will you not desist?"[18]

---

[15] *Sahih* al-Bukhari, Book 34, *Hadith* 121.
[16] *Sunan* Ibn Majah, Vol. 3 Book 12 *Hadith* 2276.
[17] Jami` at-Tirmidhi, Book 14, *Hadith* 30.
[18] *Qur'an* 5:91.

Furthermore, in commercial dealings that entail substantial risk, there is a high probability that one party will emerge as a "winner" to the detriment of the counterparty, who comes out of the transaction as a "loser." That is, the *Shari'a* envisions only win-win or lose-lose commercial relationships. For example, in the case of purchasing an unborn male calf at its market price, if the animal is stillborn, then the buyer loses. If it is born a female and is, thus, more valuable for its milk, then the seller loses having accepted a price lower than the animal's actual value. Thus, as in gambling, *gharar* transactions can lead to animosity, hatred, or – in modern society – litigation.

In the context of Islamic banking and finance, the prohibition on *gharar* does not necessarily act as an impediment to commercial and economic growth. That is, the *Shari'a* does not per se forbid risk, but only *excessive* risk. Thus, for example, leasing an asset to an individual does not necessarily entail *gharar*, even though it is impossible to know if the lessee will be faithful to the contract in the future. Rather, the forbidden element of *gharar* can be avoided simply by specifically and explicitly laying out all the terms of the lease.

2. Permissible financial instruments

To be sure, Islam encourages people to give and lend their property freely, either as an act of charity to the needy or as an expression of cooperation with and kindness to fellow humans. At the same time, Islam encourages commerce, economic growth, and personal responsibility in financial dealings. Keeping this tension in mind, it is important to understand that finance is a foundational aspect of the economy. Smart, knowledgeable, and savvy investors are invaluable to the economic growth of society because they encourage entrepreneurs and businesspeople to form innovative and useful business ideas. However, investors would soon find themselves penniless if they only engaged in gratuitous lending practices, which would eventually lead to a catastrophic breakdown of the economic system. For this reason, Islamic scholars have vehemently sought to protect the private property of investors and their right to pursue and enjoy returns on their investment activities.

While investment activities clearly involving interest and speculation are forbidden, financial instruments that seek to achieve the same result as such investments, while avoiding their forbidden elements, are permitted. The following *Shari'a*-compliant financial instruments seek to achieve such a goal. They are created by executing two or more lawful contracts under Islamic law. While contracting parties can theoretically create an endless amount of *Shari'a*-compliant financing instruments, the following popular instruments have been almost universally recognized across the Islamic legal world and are frequently used by both Islamic and non-Islamic banks.

a. Mudaraba

A *mudaraba* contract is essentially a sleeping partnership arrangement. There are at least two parties in a *mudaraba* relationship: an investor (the *rab al mal*) and an investee (the *mudarib*). The investor and investee form a partnership to operate a joint venture whereby the former acts as a sleeping partner and provides capital and the latter acts as a manager over the business activities of the joint venture.

The *mudaraba* contract is arguably the most important financial instrument in Islamic law for two reasons. First, its structure is a very effective illustration of the overall theory of Islamic finance law. Second, the *mudaraba* structure, as discussed later, provides the framework on which the majority of Islamic banks operate.

i. Forming and operating a *mudaraba* arrangement

Essentially, a *mudaraba* relationship is formed and operated in a four step process, which entails negotiations, transferring / purchasing assets, operation of the subject business, and distribution of the net profits.

1) Negotiations

First, the *rab al mal* and the *mudarib* negotiate their contract. This includes agreeing on the value of the capital to be contributed by the investor, the term of the investment relationship, the business activities to be carried out by the investee, and a fair profit sharing arrangement. Generally, the investee will be an entrepreneur with a potentially profitable business idea who is in need of funding. However, sometimes the investor has a business plan in mind and is only looking for a partner to manage the venture.

An example of an acceptable profit sharing arrangement may allocate 60 percent of profits to the investor and 40 percent of profits to the investee. As in all financial dealings in Islamic law, all of the terms of the contract must be meticulously detailed and the division of profits may not be unfairly beneficial to one party and detrimental to the counterparty. Thus, for example, a *mudaraba* contract that allocates 1 percent of profit to the investee and 99 percent to the investor would probably be unlawful.

2) Transfer / purchase of assets

After the parties have officially entered into a *mudaraba* contractual relationship, the investor will transfer her agreed upon capital contribution to the investee. Generally, the capital contribution will be wholly comprised of money, which the investee will use to purchase the assets needed to operate the joint venture. However, some investors prefer to purchase the assets themselves – perhaps to ensure that the assets are of the necessary quality or that they are purchased at the best price – and then transfer the assets to the investee.

3) Operation of the business

After the investee has obtained the assets needed to operate the joint venture, either by purchasing them with the investor's capital contribution or receiving them directly from the investor, the investee commences the business activities.

4) Distribution of net profits

In the final stage, the investee distributes the profits of the joint venture to herself and the investor according to their agreed upon profit-sharing arrangement. First, however, the costs and expenses of the joint venture must be satisfied out of the profits. Then, assuming that there is a net profit, the net profit is distributed to the parties. If there is no net profit, then neither party receives a distribution. Further, if the joint venture business has debts or liabilities that remain unsatisfied due to lack of profit, the investor is liable to pay them up to the amount of her capital contribution.

ii. Notes on *mudaraba* contracts

Isolated from reality, the *mudaraba* arrangement is a simple financial instrument on paper. In reality, however, there are many pitfalls and impediments that *mudaraba* parties can encounter. First, it is important to note that the investee retains significant control and power in the *mudaraba* relationship. For example, as a matter of law, the profits that result from the business are attributable to and accrue to the investee. While the investee is contractually bound and owes a fiduciary duty to the investor, it is ultimately the investee who distributes the investor's rightful share to her. Thus, a savvy investor will conduct a due diligence check on the investee to uncover any adverse history that would indicate a character for dishonesty or an inferior business acumen. In addition, the investor should ensure that the *mudaraba* relationship remain financially transparent by requiring that the investee agree to disclose all profit and loss statements, tax filings, and receipts to her.

Next, in many Islamic law jurisdictions, the investee's share of the *mudaraba* profits may be capped at a fixed amount. One of the most influential standard-setting bodies for Islamic finance, the Accounting and Auditing Organization for Islamic Financial Institutions (AAOIFI),[19] has approved the use of caps in this regard. For example, assume that an investor and investee enter into a *mudaraba* contract allocating 60 percent of net profits to the investor and 40 percent to the investee, with the investee's share capped at USD 100,000. Thus, if the net profits of the venture amount to USD one million, then the investee's share is capped at USD 100,000. However, if the net profits are only USD 200,000, then the investee's share would amount to USD 80,000.

Finally, it is important to note that the investor and investee are considered distinct parties under a *mudaraba* contract and their activities must be kept separate from each other. For example, the investor may only act as a silent partner. If she begins to cross the line by becoming an active partner and interfering in the daily business affairs of the venture, then the *mudaraba* contract will default to a *musharaka* (partnership) arrangement. Nevertheless, the investor can retain control over the investee's activities by ensuring that the *mudaraba* contract is meticulously written. For example, the AAOIFI notes that the investor may designate the market or sector within which the investee may purchase assets for the venture. Any use of the investor's capital contribution or the funds in the venture's expense account outside of the

---

[19] *See* ACCOUNTING AND AUDITING ORGANIZATION FOR ISLAMIC FINANCIAL INSTITUTIONS, www.aaoifi.com.

designated market or sector would constitute a breach of the *mudaraba* contract.

b. Murabaha

A *murabaha* contract is best described as a markup and resale contract. At first glance, this agreement seems to clearly involve the prohibited element of interest in the transaction. However, Islamic scholars have almost universally accepted the *murabaha* financing instrument because it is comprised of a chain of legally permissible contracts. A *murabaha* arrangement functions as follows.

i. Pre-contract negotiations

Contractual certainty is a strict requirement under Islamic law. Thus, the parties must be in complete agreement regarding their rights and duties under a *murabaha* contract. Satisfaction of this requirement usually entails a two-step process.

First, a lender and a borrower meet and agree to cooperate in the purchase of an asset that the borrower wants and / or needs but lacks the available capital to purchase by herself. For example, many *murabaha* agreements facilitate the purchase of homes and automobiles.

Second, after the borrower and lender have identified the asset for purchase and its price, they will agree upon a markup price of the asset to be paid by the borrower in installments over a period of time. As with any contract under Islamic law, the markup price and period of repayment must be meticulously detailed and may not be unfairly advantageous to one party and detrimental to the counterparty.

ii. Execution

In order for a *murabaha* agreement to be lawful, the execution thereof must follow a strict contractual process.

Proper execution of a *murabaha* agreement usually entails two legally permissible contracts. While the result of a *murabaha* agreement seems to involve interest, Islamic scholars agree that the *murabaha* agreement is permissible because the means used to achieve the result are completely lawful under the aforementioned principles of Islamic contract law.

In the first contract, the lender purchases the subject asset of the *murabaha* contract from the third-party seller. Importantly, this contract is outside of the scope of the agreement between the borrower and the lender. Thus, the lender can negotiate however she pleases with the third-party seller. However, the lender must receive full title to the asset free and clear of any liens or encumbrances.

In the second contract, the lender will resell the asset to the borrower at a markup price. This markup contract is executed by the lender's transfer of the asset to the borrower in exchange for the borrower's promise to repay the lender at a higher total price than what the lender paid for the asset.

For example, suppose that a borrower seeks financing to purchase a new automobile of a certain make and model and is willing to pay USD 500 per month for 5 years. A lender agrees to finance the purchase and determines that a car dealer is willing to sell a suitable automobile for USD 20,000. First, the lender purchases the automobile from the dealer. Then, the lender resells the automobile to the borrower for payment of USD 500 per month for 5 years, a total of USD 30,000. Assuming that the contract is properly carried out, the lender will earn USD 10,000 from the arrangement.

iii. Default

Even if a *murabaha* contract is flawlessly drafted on paper, there will always be the possibility of future circumstances that can disrupt the *murabaha* relationship in practice. When the borrower defaults on her obligation to pay, the lender has the right to foreclose on the property and retake possession.

c. Ijara

Ijara agreements are another manner in which investors can put their money to work in an Islamic economy. Essentially, the *ijara* arrangement is a contract whereby an investor purchases property to rent to a lessee in return for rental payments. Throughout the leasing contract, the investor retains title to her leased asset. Islamic scholars almost universally agree that *ijara* contracts are valid financing instruments. However, there are some limitations on their validity.

First, as noted in Chapter Two, contractual terms must be explicitly defined so as to avoid the prohibited element of excessive risk (*gharar*). Thus, the rental period, description of the asset, and rental payments due to the lessor must be clearly and unequivocally expressed in the contract.

Next, in order to establish the elements of fairness and equity in commercial dealings which Islamic law seeks to achieve, the investor must bear some of the risk in an *ijara* relationship. In an *ijara* contract, the investor retains title to the leased property while the lessee holds possession of the property's usufruct. Thus, the investor remains liable for the costs of owning the property and for repairs stemming from the lessee's possession of the property.

Upon the termination of the *ijara* contract at the close of the rental period or upon the lessee's default under the arrangement, the lessee's right to possess the property ends and such right is transferred to the investor. Alternatively, in a similar *ijara wa iqtina* (lease to own) agreement, a portion of the lessee's rental payment is applied toward an agreed upon purchase price of the leased asset. Upon satisfaction of the purchase price, title to the asset transfers from the investor to the lessee.

d. Salam

A *salam* agreement is a prepayment instrument for the future delivery of goods, which bears similarities to the concept of futures. Essentially, an investor pays a seller a set price for goods to be delivered at some point in the future. The investor is hoping that the value of the goods appreciates when the time of delivery arrives so that she can immediately resell them for a profit.

This concept is easiest to illustrate in an agricultural context. For example, assume that the market value of dates is ten dirhams per bushel today. An investor approaches a farmer and offers to pay her today for the delivery of one thousand bushels of dates in one year at today's market price. The farmer, induced by the promise of immediate payment, agrees. When delivery is made next year, the investor hopes that the market price of dates has exceeded ten dirhams per bushel, thereby allowing for the possibility of reselling the dates at a higher price than what she had paid one year prior.

At first glance, this type of transaction – especially transactions involving nonexistent goods – seems to involve excessive risk. However, the prohibited element of *gharar* in *salam* instruments can be avoided by ensuring that all contractual terms (e.g., price, delivery date, quality, quantity, etc.) are explicitly and particularly laid out.

In the unfortunate scenario that the seller fails to perform under the *salam* contract and deliver the goods, the investor is limited to two remedies. First, she can allow the seller more time to deliver. Alternatively, she can demand restitution of the exact amount of her investment, and no more.

C. Islamic Banking

As aforementioned, Islamic banking is a booming industry and an important topic under Islamic law. Indeed, the recent increase in the influence of Islamic banking can be measured in both dollar signs and geographical reach. For example, Islamic banks and Islamic banking branches of many well-known global, conventional banks can be found all throughout the Middle East and in parts of Africa and Asia.[20] However, conventional banks operating in regions such as Europe, the United States, and Canada also offer *Shari'a*-compliant banking services in addition to conventional banking services.[21]

Notwithstanding the importance and influence of Islamic banking throughout the world, the structure and operation of an Islamic bank is fairly simple. Despite this simplicity, however, the Islamic banking sector is subject to certain unique challenges that most conventional banks do not face.

1. Structure

In general, most Islamic banks operate on the structure of the aforementioned *mudaraba* financial instrument. However, in the *mudaraba* banking model, Islamic banks fulfill dual roles by acting as both investor and investee. That is, an Islamic bank is essentially a two-tiered *mudaraba* arrangement which involves the bank as well as both depositors and borrowers.

---

[20] For example, HSBC Amanah currently operates in Saudi Arabia and Malaysia, while JP Morgan offers Islamic banking services in Bahrain, Egypt, Lebanon, Saudi Arabia, and the United Arab Emirates.

[21] For example, University Bank – located in Ann Arbor, Michigan – maintains an Islamic banking services branch, while American Finance House Lariba – based in Pasadena, California – works with banks all over the United States to offer certain *Shari'a*-compliant banking services. Further, the Islamic Bank of Britain offers *Shari'a*-compliant banking services for its clients in the United Kingdom.

a. Tier one

On the first tier, the depositors act as the *rab al mal* by investing funds with the bank, which acts as the *mudarib*. All of the applicable rules of the *mudaraba* contractual relationship apply on this first tier in the way that they would in a normal *mudaraba* relationship. For example, the terms of the investment relationship – including the profit sharing ratio, amount of the depositor's investment, and the term of the investment – must be meticulously detailed and laid out for both parties to understand.

However, there are certain default rules that will always apply in the first tier relationship. For example, it is understood that the joint venture/business activity over which the bank will act as manager will be wholly comprised of *Shari'a*-compliant banking and financing activities. However, depositors can choose to place their funds in accounts that invest the funds therein in certain, specific activities. For example, an Islamic bank may offer investment accounts that provide lower, yet more certain, returns that only invest in less risky financing activities, such as *murabaha* agreements. On the other hand, the bank may offer investment accounts that offer the possibility of higher returns by investing the account's funds in riskier financing instruments, such as *mudaraba* agreements.

In the same way that the *mudarib* is not obligated to make a distribution of funds to the *rab al mal* when the joint venture fails to realize a net profit in a single tier *mudaraba* relationship, the bank is not obligated to pay returns on depositors' accounts when the accounts are unprofitable. Furthermore, absent gross and willful negligence, the bank cannot be held liable for the total loss of depositors' funds.

b. Tier two

On the second tier, the Islamic bank switches character and essentially becomes a *rab al mal* by investing deposited funds with borrowers. However, the relationship between the bank and the borrowers is not always a *mudaraba* arrangement and the labels "*rab al mal*" and "*mudarib*" do not strictly apply to the bank and the borrowers, respectively, because the bank can enter into any profit-generating financial instrument that complies with Islamic law. For example, the vast majority of investment activity that takes place on the second tier level of most Islamic banks is comprised of *murabaha* agreements. This is essentially due to the fact that *murabaha* financing tends to offer the most desirable balance between risk and reward. However, the second tier investment activity of an Islamic bank can involve any Islamic financial instrument, including the aforementioned examples. Further, with approval from the bank's *Shari'a* board, Islamic banks can create any financial product and offer it to borrowers.

2. Challenges in the Islamic banking sector

While the structure of Islamic banking appears to be clear and simple, the Islamic banking sector is subject to certain drawbacks and impediments. Specifically, Islamic banks suffer from certain competitive pressures as well as excessive bureaucratic expense and inefficiency related to its product approval process.

a. Challenges related to competition with conventional banks

To begin, in a dual-banking jurisdiction that allows both Islamic and conventional banking and financing activities, Islamic banks are subject to competitive pressures referred to as "displaced commercial risk" (DCR). This challenge entails:

the risk of losses which an Islamic bank absorbs to make sure that . . . depositors are paid a rate of return equivalent to a benchmark or a competitive rate of return . . . as a result of commercial pressure or regulatory pressure.[22]

Under the Islamic banking model based on the *mudaraba* financing instrument, deposits are not guaranteed and depositors cannot be certain that their investments will see a return. On the other hand, conventional banks can offer accounts that guarantee depositors an interest-based return. Therefore,

under commercial pressure, the majority of Islamic banks smooth the rate of return attributed to their [depositors] at the expense of profits normally attributed to shareholders in order to offer them a competitive remuneration and persuade them to keep their funds in the bank.[23]

If left uncontrolled, DCR can lead to the total collapse of an Islamic bank. Thus, Islamic banks operating in a dual-banking jurisdiction are left with a perplexing dilemma. That is, they can offer returns wholly indicative of their financial activities and risk losing customers when the returns are low, or they can smooth their returns in times when business is unproductive and risk collapse.

In addition to competitive challenges related to DCR from operating in a dual-banking jurisdiction, Islamic banks can also fail to fulfill the purpose of Islamic banking and finance due to competitive pressures. For example, because of the low-risk, high-reward nature of the *murabaha* (markup sale)

---

[22] KAOUTHER TOUMI, JEAN-LAURENT VIVIANI, AND LOTFI BELKACEM, FINANCE AND SUSTAINABILITY: TOWARDS A NEW PARADIGM? A POST-CRISIS AGENDA 325, (Emerald 2011) (William Sun, Celine Louche, and Roland Perez, eds.).

[23] *Id.*

financing instrument, "[Islamic] banks rely on *murabaha* for some eighty percent of their investments, while *mudaraba* [sleeping partnership] is nearly always below five percent."[24] While the *murabaha* instrument is a useful and approved financing method, its usefulness is generally limited to the purchase of assets such as homes and cars. On the other hand, the *mudaraba* arrangement, while riskier, can contribute to significant economic development depending on the success of the business model. However, Islamic banks must be able to compete, which requires satisfying depositors' demands for investment returns. Thus, Islamic banks are more inclined to focus on offering highly predictable and less risky *murabaha* loans.

b. Challenges related to product approval

In addition to commercially competitive pressures on Islamic banks, the Islamic banking sector suffers from bureaucratic inefficiency in the approval of financial products and the expense associated with maintaining experts to sit on product approval boards.

First, any financial product marketed by an Islamic bank must undergo a rigorous two-step analysis. The first step is an internal examination and is carried out at the level of the Islamic bank. Specifically, the bank's *Shari'a* board will issue a *fatwa* approving or denying the product. Next, the second step is an external examination and occurs at the level of the Central Bank or other banking regulator in the bank's jurisdiction. Assuming that the financial product passes both steps of this rigorous analysis, it can be put on the market.

However, international Islamic banking and finance standardizing bodies require that all financial products undergo the same rigorous analysis, even if the product has

---

[24] FRANK VOGEL AND SAMUEL HAYES, III, ISLAMIC FINANCE: RELIGION, RISK AND RETURN 135, (Kluwer 1998).

been approved before or is substantially similar to another approved product. For example, the Islamic Financial Services Board states,

> Shari'a scholars in each locality should arrive at their own opinions that can address appropriately and effectively the specific problems of the [community] within their respective localities. . . . Although the diversity of Shari'a opinions might tempt an [Islamic Bank] to adhere to the fatwa of other Shari'a scholars at the expense of differing fatwa issued by the [Islamic Bank]'s Shari'a scholars, the [Islamic Bank] shall not change their allegiance and obedience to fatwa to suit their convenience. Such a practice could impair the independence of Shari'a scholars and have a damaging impact on the integrity and credibility of the individual [Islamic Bank], in particular, and on the Islamic financial services industry as a whole.[25]

Next, in addition to the difficulties associated with obtaining a two-part approval for each financial product, the expenses required for maintaining a Shari'a board for an Islamic bank's internal analysis can be significant. The task of the Shari'a board is to examine the financial product under development, determine if its transactional structure complies with Islamic law, and issue a fatwa stating its findings. A fatwa is "a juristic opinion that is accepted as definitive. Such an opinion can be issued only by a recognized Islamic legal authority. . . . That authority is the mufti in the Sunnite world, or an Ayatollah in the Shi'ite world."[26] A mufti is "[a] specialist in Islamic Law who is accredited, by virtue of outstanding

---

[25] ISLAMIC FINANCIAL SERVICES BOARD, GUIDING PRINCIPLES ON CORPORATE GOVERNANCE FOR INSTITUTIONS OFFERING ONLY ISLAMIC FINANCIAL SERVICES (EXCLUDING ISLAMIC INSURANCE (TAKAFUL) INSTITUTIONS AND ISLAMIC MUTUAL FUNDS), ¶¶ 45 – 54.

[26] RAJ BHALA, UNDERSTANDING ISLAMIC LAW (SHARI'A) 1401 (Lexis Nexis 2011).

scholarly reputation and personal piety, governmental authority, or both, to give an authoritative legal opinion."[27]

There are ten requirements that an individual must achieve in order to attain the status of *mufti*. Specifically, the individual must have an ultimate awareness of legislating Quranic verses, knowledge of the *Sunnah* and the reliability of its narrators, knowledge of the rules of abrogation and abrogated rules, knowledge of *Ijma* (consensus) as a source of law, knowledge of the secondary sources of Islamic law, an understanding of analogical reasoning, a mastery of the Arabic language, an understanding of the five objectives of the *Shari'a* (which are property, prosperity, lineage, life, and religion), knowledge of the specific situation for which she issues a *fatwa* and, finally, a *mufti* must have a disposition of piety.[28] Given the time and expense associated with the studies that are necessary for an individual to undertake in order to attain the status of *mufti*, an Islamic bank must expend significant resources in order to hire qualified individuals to sit on its *Shari'a* board as *mufti*. This factor can cut into the profits of Islamic banks to the detriment of depositors.

D. *SHARI'A*-COMPLIANT SECURITIES

A recent trend in Islamic financing involves the use of Islamic bonds, which are *Shari'a*-compliant securities, to provide funding to investees and a stream of income to investors. The bonds, which are called *sukuk*, can be privately issued and held. Alternatively, the *sukuk* can be publicly listed and traded in secondary capital markets. The structure of *sukuk* financing is most often based on the *mudaraba* and *ijara*

---

[27] *Id.* at 1426.

[28] MOHAMMAD HASHIM KAMALI, PRINCIPLES OF ISLAMIC JURISPRUDENCE (1999); *see also* MOHAMMAD HASHIM KAMALI, SHARI'AH LAW: AN INTRODUCTION (2008).

financing instruments. In both cases, however, the use of an intermediary third party is necessary. The intermediary can be a special purpose vehicle (SPV) set up by the investors and the investee. However, banks often offer *sukuk* financing services by acting as intermediary in return for a fee.

The universal structure of *sukuk* financing involves a four step process. First, the investee(s) will call on investors to assist with the financing of an asset or assets in return for payment. Second, the parties will approach a bank or create an SPV. The bank or SPV will issue *sukuk* certificates to the investors in return for capital contributions. Third, the SPV or bank will use the funds to purchase the asset or assets. Finally, the bank or SPV will execute a financial arrangement with the investee(s), which is often based on either the *mudaraba* or *ijara* financing instruments (*supra*).

1. *Sukuk al-mudaraba*

In the case of *sukuk al-mudaraba*, the bank or SPV executes a *mudaraba* contract with the investee(s) whereby the asset or assets are sold to the investee(s) in return for a percentage of net profits from their use of the asset or assets. For example, assume that an investee is a hotel operator and seeks to finance a new hotel. The willing investors will contribute capital to the bank or SPV in return for *sukuk al-mudaraba* certificates. Then, the bank or SPV will use the funds from the contribution to build or purchase the hotel. Next, the bank or SPV will execute a *mudaraba* contract with the investee whereby the bank or SPV receives, for example, 60 percent of the net profits of the operation of the hotel and the investee receives 40 percent.

All of the aforementioned rules governing the *mudaraba* relationship will apply. That is, if there is no net profit, then neither the bank / SPV, the investors, nor the investee receives a distribution. However, assuming there is a net profit, the bank or SPV will distribute its share to the *sukuk al-mudaraba* certificate holders pro rata. But if the intermediary is a bank, it will also take a percentage of the investors' share as a fee. In contrast to the *sukuk al-ijara* structure (*see infra*), *sukuk al-mudaraba* are riskier. Depending on the investment, the return could be significantly high or substantially low.

2. *Sukuk al-ijara*

In the case of *sukuk al-ijara*, the bank or SPV executes an *ijara* contract with the investee(s) whereby the asset or assets are leased to the investee(s) in return for fixed rental payments. For example, assume again that an investee is a hotel operator and seeks to finance a new hotel. The willing investors will contribute capital to the bank or SPV in return for *sukuk al-ijara* certificates. Then, the bank or SPV will use the funds from the contribution to build or purchase the hotel. Next, the bank or SPV will execute an *ijara* contract with the investee whereby the bank or SPV holds title to the hotel and leases it to the investee. Finally, the bank or SPV will distribute the lease payments to the investors pro rata.

In contrast to the *sukuk al-mudaraba* structure, the *sukuk al-ijara* certificate holders know the exact amount of the return that they will receive on their investment – assuming that the investee does not default on the lease. In this regard, all of the aforementioned rules governing the *ijara* relationship will apply. That is, if the investee defaults on rent, the bank or SPV may repossess the hotel, sell it off, and distribute the proceeds to the investors.

CHAPTER 5. FAMILY LAW

A. INTRODUCTION

The family unit is the basic building block of society. As such, the community is benefitted when family ties hold together and function well. When the basic family unit is stable, all of its members are better equipped to contribute to the local political, religious, and economic functions of everyday life. Notwithstanding theories of freedom of choice, the ability to legislate morality, and the increasingly important arguments concerning women's rights under Islam, the law acts as both a deterrent for perceived harmful behavior and an incentive for perceived positive behavior. As such, Islamic law provides guidelines for matters related to the functioning of the family unit in the areas of marriage, divorce, and children.

B. MARRIAGE

According to Islam, marriage is considered more of an act of worship to God than a solely transactional relationship. The purpose of marriage is generally based in romantic ideals of love and attraction. However, the legal rules governing marriage are based on theories of contractual freedom and morality. In any case, Islamic law maintains certain requirements for a marriage contract to be valid and binding, prescribes rights and duties for the parties to a marriage contract, and restricts the freedom to marry in certain circumstances.

1. Requirements for a valid marriage contract

First, as in any contractual undertaking, an offer and acceptance is required to form a valid marriage contract. That is, one person must express an offer to enter into a marital relationship and the other person must accept the offer. It is important to note that these contractual elements must comply with Islamic contract law (*see supra* Chapter Two). Thus, the parties must, for example, have capacity to create a contract. However, guardians can enter into marital contracts on behalf of minors who lack capacity. In any case, as part of the evidentiary requirements for creating a valid marriage contract, the offer and acceptance must be attested by two Muslim witnesses.

Next, the parties must agree on an acceptable dowry (*mahr*) to be paid to the bride by the groom. The dowry can be anything that has value under Islamic law, including money or property. That is, it must be a *halaal* (permissible) object or it must come from a *halaal* source of wealth under the large umbrella of Islam. Further, the parties can agree to an immediate or deferred payout of the dowry. However, the bride will always have a right to any unpaid portion of the dowry, even after divorce, and she has the right to withhold her marital duties (*see infra*) if the groom unduly delays in paying all or part of the dowry.

Next, it is important to note that the foregoing elements are strictly required in order to create a binding marital contract. If any of the elements are missing, then the marriage contract is voidable at either party's discretion. However, any children produced from the voidable relationship are considered to be legitimate (i.e., the man in the voidable relationship is considered the father of the child).

Finally, Islamic tradition holds that the marriage ceremony should be conducted and announced in public in a mosque and, further, that the families of the newlyweds should provide a meal, called a *waliemah*, soon after the ceremony. The families are required to invite all people from the community, both rich and poor, to the *waliemah* meal and invitees must have a compelling reason to refuse attendance.

2. Rights and duties under the marriage contract

Throughout the marriage relationship, the husband and wife must remain committed to each other financially, physically, and emotionally. Adultery, which is defined as any voluntary sexual activity outside marital bonds, can be severely punished under the criminal law (*see infra* Chapter Six).

First, the husband has a duty to provide *nafaka* (maintenance) to his wife all throughout the marriage relationship. This includes providing food, clothing, and shelter according to his financial means. Importantly, the husband must individually own the housing which he offers as shelter to his wife. That is, he cannot share housing with others and compel his wife to join him in the shared housing.

Next, it is important to note that Islamic law recognizes the common law doctrine of necessaries. That is, if a husband fails to fulfill his marital duty of providing maintenance, his wife may purchase necessaries against his credit. In doing so, the husband becomes liable for his wife's purchases, but only to the extent that the purchases are made for basic necessities.

Next, the wife has a duty to obey and respect her husband. In this regard, a husband has the right to correct and punish his wife when she refuses to fulfill this duty. Generally, a husband only exercises this right as a last resort. For example, the *Qur'an* states,

> Men are in charge of women by [right of] what Allah has given one over the other and what they spend [for maintenance] from their wealth. So righteous women are devoutly obedient, guarding in [the husband's]

absence what Allah would have them guard. But those [wives] from whom you fear arrogance - [first] advise them; [then if they persist], forsake them in bed; and [finally], strike them. But if they obey you [once more], seek no means against them.[29]

Thus, a husband should only resort to physical violence against his wife after using words and withholding conjugal relations has failed to restore marital harmony. However, many of the Prophet Muhammad's (PBUH) teachings in the *Sunnah* show that inflicting violence on one's wife is highly disfavored. For example, Muhammad said, "[t]he most perfect man in his faith among the believers is the one whose behavior is most excellent; and the best of you are those who are the best to their wives."[30] Further, whenever beating is justified, it should not be inflicted on the face. Muhammad said, "[i]f a person beats somebody, then he should avoid the face."[31]

Finally, the wife has a right to seek education and the husband has a duty to provide her with the necessary resources to receive an education. Similarly, the wife has a right to earn her own income by engaging in business or seeking employment. All of the income which she receives belongs to her alone as separate property.

3. Restrictions on marriage

Islamic law restricts the ability for certain individuals to marry each other based on certain characteristics, including familial relations, religious association, and gender.

---

[29] *Qur'an* 4:34.
[30] Riyad Al Salihin, Book 1, *Hadith* 628.
[31] *Sahih* Al Bukhari, Book 49, *Hadith* 42.

a. Blood and foster relations

Islamic law prohibits marriage on the basis of blood relations, whether full or half blood related. Specifically, persons are prohibited from marrying the following blood relatives:

- Grandparents, great-grandparents, etc.;
- Siblings of grandparents (i.e., great-aunts and great-uncles);
- Parents (and certain foster mothers);
- Siblings of parents (i.e., aunts and uncles);
- Siblings;
- Sons and daughters;
- Nieces and nephews; and
- Grandchildren, great-grandchildren, etc.

Note that marriage between cousins is not prohibited on the basis of blood relations restrictions. Further, Islamic law forbids marrying a foster mother in certain circumstances. Specifically, if a man fed five times from a woman's breast as a child, he is forbidden from marrying her later.

b. Other restrictions

Under Islamic law, polygyny is permitted in certain circumstances, while polyandry is forbidden. Put differently, a man is allowed to have more than one wife – but no more than four wives – at any given time while a woman may only have one husband at a time. However, the conditions required for polygyny are stringent. Namely, the husband must be able to sufficiently fulfill all of his marital duties (*see supra*) to each wife equally. Further, it is recommended that a husband get permission from his existing wife before marrying a second wife. Finally, a husband may not marry closely related relatives of his existing wife or wives (i.e., his wife's mother, sister, or daughter).

Marriage is also restricted on the basis of religion, gender, and in certain cases of divorce. First, a Muslim woman may only marry a Muslim man. However, a Muslim man may marry a woman who is Muslim, Christian, or Jewish. Next, homosexual relations are strictly forbidden in Islam. In the same way, marriage between persons of the same gender is prohibited. Finally, in the case of an irrevocable divorce (*see infra*), remarriage between the former spouses is generally forbidden. The exception to this rule is when the ex-wife marries another man, who either dies or divorces her. Thereafter, the former spouses can remarry despite having had an irrevocable divorce.

C. DIVORCE

Generally, the commitment of marriage is considered to be a serious undertaking in Islamic culture. However, certain marital relationships simply do not work out, whether due to the fault of either or both spouses or, alternatively, due to unknown reasons that cannot be contributed to wrongdoing. Thus, the community is best served by a legal system that provides for a fair and just mechanism for dissolving an unwanted matrimonial relationship.

At the outset, it is important to note that the underlying rationale for essentially all of Islamic family law is to ensure that paternity can be ascertained for all children. In this way, courts are able to pin the responsibility of parenthood on men who father children. Further, establishing paternity is important for purposes of Islamic inheritance law. For this reason, whenever a woman divorces a man or becomes a widow, she must engage in a waiting period, called an *iddat*. The waiting period in the case of a divorced woman is three menstrual cycles, whereas the waiting period for a widow is four months and ten days. In either case, however, if the woman is pregnant, her *iddat* lasts for as long as her pregnancy lasts. That is, the *iddat* period terminates when she gives birth, which could either decrease or increase the *iddat* period. For example, if a woman is divorced or widowed at a time when she was in the last week of her pregnancy, then the woman's *iddat* period would only last one week. On the other hand, if a woman is divorced or widowed one week after having conceived, then her *iddat* period would last somewhere around nine months.

During the *iddat* period, the woman must remain in her house and may not leave. This is a method which is used to ensure that, if it turns out that she is pregnant upon divorce or upon the death of her husband, the paternity of the child can be unquestionably established because there was (probably) no chance for her to engage in sexual relations with another man. Upon the culmination of the *iddat* period for a divorcee, the dissolution of the marriage becomes effective and the ex-spouses are free to remarry. In the same way, when a widow completes her *iddat*, she is free to remarry whomever she pleases.

With the advent of scientific technology and DNA testing capabilities, the need for the *iddat* period is subject to wide debate. However, traditionalists note that the *iddat* requirement allows for a necessary time period in which a widow can mourn the loss of her husband, while stubborn and embittered spouses can spend time apart from each other to evaluate and reconsider their relationship. Because the divorce is not official until the *iddat* ends, the parties can rejoin before the *iddat* expires without any consequences.

1. Requirements for dissolution of marriage

The *Shari'a* imposes different requirements on men and women when either party seeks a divorce. Under Islamic law, a man can obtain a divorce from his wife by way of issuing *talaaq* – which means "repudiation" in Arabic – to her. On the other hand, a woman is limited to seeking divorce by requesting her husband to issue *talaaq* to her, petitioning a court to issue *talaaq* on her behalf, or performing *khul'a*, which entails offering to pay compensation for a divorce.

a. Talaaq

A man's right to dissolve marital ties with his wife is governed by the rules of *talaaq*. There are three different forms of *talaaq* by which a man may seek divorce from his wife. However, the effectiveness of issuing *talaaq* entails certain formalities and procedural actions. Further, once *talaaq* is issued, the spouses are subject to certain consequences.

i. Methods of dissolving the marriage through *talaaq*.

A man may issue *talaaq* in three different ways. Each method essentially reaches the same result, which is dissolution of the marital relationship. However, the first method, *talaaq ahsan*, is considered to be the most favorable, while *talaaq bid'ee* is extremely disfavored. On the other hand, *talaaq hasan* is neither favored nor disfavored, but is simply acceptable.

1) Talaaq ahsan

In *talaaq ahsan*, the man issues *talaaq* during his wife's pure period (i.e., while she is not menstruating). Thereafter, the man must abstain from cohabiting or engaging in sexual intercourse with her. Next, the woman begins her *iddat* (waiting period), which ends after completion of three menstrual cycles or until she gives birth. After completion of the *iddat*, the marriage is formally dissolved and the woman is permitted to remarry.

2) Talaaq hasan

In *talaaq hasan*, the man issues *talaaq* to his wife in three consecutive periods of non-menstruating purity. As an example, and for purposes of clarity, assume the woman completes a menstrual cycle on 1 January. Then, on 2 January, the man issues *talaaq*. Next, the woman completes a second menstrual cycle on 1 February and, on 2 February, the man issues a second *talaaq*. Finally, on 1 March, the woman completes a third menstrual cycle and, on 2 March, the marriage is officially dissolved after the man issues a third *talaaq*.

It is important to note two points of *talaaq hasan*. First, immediately after issuing the first words of *talaaq* on 2 January, the man must abstain from cohabitating or engaging in sexual intercourse with his wife. In this way, if the woman turns out to be pregnant, the paternity of the child can be established. Second, Islamic law generally forbids ex-spouses to remarry each other after the husband has issued a total of three *talaaqs* (*see infra*) Thus, *talaaq hasan* is not a favorable method of divorce because it restricts the ex-spouse's ability to remarry in the future.

3) Talaaq bid'ee

While considered to be a sinful act, issuing *talaaq bid'ee* is nevertheless effective to dissolve a marriage. In *talaaq bid'ee*, the man issues a disfavored *talaaq* in one of three ways.

a) Issuing *talaaq* more than once in one sitting

The first instance of *talaaq bid'ee* occurs by issuing words of *talaaq* two or three times in one sentence. For example, saying "I divorce you, I divorce you, I divorce you" or "I give you two *talaaqs*" constitutes a *talaaq bid'ee*. This method of divorce is disfavored because it is unnecessary and often occurs out of anger. That is, one *talaaq* is sufficient to begin the dissolution process and issuing more *talaaqs* than necessary out of anger is evidence of a lack of self-control. After three statements of *talaaq*, the spouses generally cannot remarry in the future (*see infra*).

b) Issuing *talaaq* during a state of menstruation

The next instance of *talaaq bid'ee* occurs when a man issues *talaaq* during his wife's menstrual period. This method of divorce is disfavored mainly because the wife's *iddat* period does not begin to run until her next menstrual period, thus prolonging the waiting period by one month and delaying her ability to remarry.

c) Issuing *talaaq* after sexual intercourse

The final instance of *talaaq bid'ee* occurs when a man issues *talaaq* during his wife's pure period (i.e., between menstrual cycles) and after having engaged in sexual relations with her. This method of divorce is disfavored because, if a child was conceived as a result of having engaged in sexual intercourse with her husband, the wife's *iddat* period will potentially be prolonged by six months (i.e., until birth).

ii. Formalities of issuing *talaaq*

Revocation of marriage by *talaaq* must strictly be issued with words either orally or in writing. That is, a husband's demand for divorce cannot be implied in fact by his conduct. However, the words used in issuing *talaaq* can be express or implied. For example, the words "I divorce you" or "I give you *talaaq*" are sufficient to begin the process of dissolution of the marriage. However, the words "you are alone" or "count your *iddat*" are also sufficient. In any case, the man must be sane, conscious, awake, and not under any duress when issuing the words of *talaaq*. Importantly, *talaaq* issued in a state of intoxication, anger, or while joking is valid and sufficient to trigger the dissolution process. Thus, the *Shari'a* encourages husbands to be careful with their words.

iii. Consequences of divorce by *talaaq*

After issuing *talaaq* to a woman one or two times, whether in one occurrence or over the course of two separate marriages, a man can revoke the *talaaq* and remarry the woman. If he revokes the *talaaq* before the woman's *iddat* expires, then no formalities are required. If, however, he issues *talaaq* to a woman and her *iddat* period expires – thus officially dissolving the marriage relationship – the man's option to revoke the *talaaq* is lost and the parties must execute a new marriage contract, which includes the requirement of a new dowry, marital contract, *waliemah*, and so on.

After a man issues *talaaq* to a woman a total of three times, he cannot remarry her unless she marries another man who either dies or divorces her. This rule applies equally whether the *talaaq* is issued three times in one occurrence or if *talaaq* is issued over the course of three separate marriages between the same parties. In any case, the parties can only remarry each other if the woman marries another man who dies or divorces her.

A revocation of the marriage contract by issuing *talaaq* does not result in the dissolution of the marriage relationship until the woman's *iddat* period expires. As such, the husband remains liable for a woman's maintenance (*see supra*) until her *iddat* period is over and the marriage is officially dissolved.

b. Women's right to divorce

A woman can seek divorce from her husband in three ways. In the first manner, a woman can divorce her husband by asking him to issue *talaaq*. In this circumstance, all of the rules governing the methods by which the husband exercises his right of divorce apply (*see supra*). The effectiveness of this manner of dissolution by the wife's request is based wholly upon the discretion of the husband. If he refuses to grant his wife's request for *talaaq*, she may perform *khul'a* (compensational divorce) or petition a judge for dissolution.

i. Divorce for compensation

Khul'a is a method in which a wife can divorce her husband by paying compensation to him. In this circumstance, the spouses will settle upon an agreeable amount as compensation. If the circumstances leading to the divorce are the fault of the husband, he should not require the woman to pay anything as compensation. On the other hand, if the circumstances leading to divorce are the fault of the wife, the husband should not accept any compensation that exceeds the value of the dowry which he paid or promised to pay to her at the beginning of the marriage. In any case, if the husband failed to fulfill his contractual obligation to effect transfer of the dowry to his wife, the wife is not obligated to pay any amount in *khul'a*.

When required, the amount to be paid in compensation to the husband will generally be expressed in terms of the value of the dowry agreed upon by both spouses at the outset of the marriage. Thus, for example, a wife seeking dissolution may offer to repay half of the value of the dowry that has been fully paid by the husband. On the other hand, a wife seeking dissolution may offer to forgive the remaining amount of a deferred dowry. In any case, if the husband agrees and accepts the amount, the marriage will be dissolved.

Should a man refuse to release his wife from the marriage contract in return for compensation, the wife may petition a judge to intervene (*see infra*). If the judge finds that the wife is entitled to be released from the marriage contract, he will either order an appropriate amount to be paid as *khul'a* or issue *talaaq* on behalf of the husband (*see infra*).

Finally, it is important to note that a dissolution of the marriage by way of *khul'a* counts as one *talaaq* in the relationship of the parties. Thus, they can remarry each other in the future as long as they have not already divorced each other two times.

ii. Divorce by court order

Next, a woman may petition a judge to intervene on her behalf when her husband refuses to divorce her by issuing *talaaq* or by accepting *khul'a*. In this circumstance, the judge may issue *talaaq* and begin the process of marital dissolution on behalf of the woman's husband, order the husband to accept an appropriate amount in *khul'a*, or simply dissolve the marriage altogether.

When a judge intervenes in a marital relationship in this way, he is permitted to take certain factors into consideration when deciding whether or not the wife's request for dissolution of the marriage should be granted. Behavior and circumstances that warrant dissolution of the marriage at the wife's request include:

- imprisonment of her husband for five or more years;
- absence of her husband for four or more years;
- impotence;
- maltreatment;
- failure to fulfill marital duties (e.g., *nafaka*, maintenance, etc. *see supra*); and
- apostasy (i.e., if her husband converts from Islam).

When the judge finds that any of the foregoing circumstances apply, the wife is entitled to divorce her husband if she desires regardless of the husband's wishes. Further, she is not obligated to return any portion of her dowry and her ex-husband remains liable to her for any unpaid portion of the dowry after the divorce.

2. The disposition of property upon dissolution

Unlike many common law and civil law jurisdictions, the *Shari'a* does not recognize any specific requirements for dividing the assets of either spouse upon the dissolution of their marriage. Under Islamic law, each spouse is considered to own property separately from the other during the marital relationship. Thus, each spouse is permitted to leave the marriage with all property that he or she owned prior to the marriage and / or obtained during the marriage.

D. CHILDREN

Perhaps the most important policy consideration behind Islamic family law concerns the treatment and disposition of children. This includes mainly making sure that a child's father can be ascertained, thus assuring that the community can hold him accountable for the care of his child. However, establishing paternity also has important implications for inheritance rights. Further, Islamic law seeks to assure that children are properly raised in a family environment envisioned according to the principles of Islam.

1. Rights and duties of parents

Both parents have a duty to raise their children correctly in accordance with the religious principles and teachings of Islam. Further, children have a duty to obey and respect their parents at all times. With that said, fathers and mothers have certain specific rights and duties under Islamic law based largely on traditional gender roles as envisioned according to the *Shari'a*.

a. Fathers

First, fathers are not permitted to practice favoritism, either in a material or emotional sense, amongst their children based on age or gender. This aspect of Islamic law represents one example of a significant change that Islam brought to the Arabian Gulf and the practices of pre-Islamic cultures. Whereas several pre-Islamic cultures favored the firstborn son over all other children, the *Shari'a* requires equality amongst all offspring. For example, Jewish law states,

> If a man has two wives, and he loves one but not the other, and both bear him sons but the firstborn is the son of the wife he does not love, when he wills his property to his sons . . . [h]e must acknowledge the son of his unloved wife as the firstborn by giving him a double share of all he has. That son is the first sign of his father's strength. The right of the firstborn belongs to him.[32]

Contrarily, Islamic law recognizes no such right that is owed to a firstborn or otherwise special descendant.

Next, fathers are required to provide their children with maintenance similar to that which husbands must provide to their wives. That is, a father must provide his children with food, clothing, and shelter according to his financial means. Generally, a father's duty to take care of his children in this regard depends upon the gender of each child. That is, a father must provide maintenance to his son until the son reaches an age of maturity wherein he is capable of working and earning an income. On the other hand, a father is required to provide maintenance to his daughter until the daughter gets married.

b. Mothers

Next, mothers under Islamic law have a duty to nurture and provide care to their children. Specifically, women must see to the proper nutrition of their children, including breastfeeding, up to the age of two years. However, women also have certain rights to custody of their children in the case of divorce (*see infra*).

2. Child custody upon divorce

In the case of divorce, all rights and duties of parenthood remain binding and intact despite the separation of the

---

[32] Deuteronomy 21:15-17 (New International Version).

mother and father. That is, all aspects of legal custody – the ability to control, make decisions for, and raise the child – continue to be shared between the former spouses. Specifically, the father is still required to continue to provide maintenance to his sons until they are able to work and earn an income and to his daughters until they are married. Further, the mother must cooperate with the father to ensure that the children are raised according to the religious beliefs and teachings of Islam.

In the application of physical custody, however, Islamic law adheres to a strict interpretation of the tender years presumption which prevailed at common law. Under the tender years presumption, courts presumed that the mother in a custody dispute should be awarded custody of her young children due to the natural relationship of care and affection between them. Thus, if the father sought custody of the child, he bore the burden of persuading the court that he was better suited to raise his young children than their mother. However, the tender years presumption has generally not stood the test of time, especially in many U.S. jurisdictions.[33]

Under Islamic law, the tender years concept is not just a presumption but is a legal right held by the mother. Specifically, mothers have the right to retain physical custody of their sons until the age of seven years. On the other hand, mothers have the right to retain physical custody of daughters until the age of nine years. Thereafter, the right to physical custody of the children transfers to the father. However, once the child experiences puberty, the child may choose with which parent he or she prefers to live. In any

---

[33] *See e.g.*, Devine v. Devine, 398 So. 2d 686 (Alabama 1981) (finding that the application of the tender years presumption in a child custody dispute violated the Equal Protection Clause of the Fourteenth Amendment of the United States Constitution because it discriminatorily and unfairly imposed an unequal burden on the father seeking custody.).

case, if a mother ever refuses physical custody of her children, the father of the children is obliged to take physical custody.

CHAPTER 6. CRIMINAL LAW AND PROCEDURE

A. INTRODUCTION

In common law and civil law jurisdictions, the criminal law is generally enforced by a public prosecutor who acts on behalf of the people within her jurisdiction. On the other hand, civil lawsuits stemming from behavior that also qualifies as criminal activity are brought by the victim or, if the victim is deceased, her estate or family. For example, when one person murders another person in a common law jurisdiction, the prosecutor will file charges against the accused on behalf of the state or all the people within that jurisdiction. Further, the prosecutor will look to the criminal code to petition the court for a criminal punishment that only the state can invoke, such as the death penalty or jail time. On the other hand, the family of the victim can bring a civil lawsuit against the accused murderer based on the jurisdiction's tort jurisprudence asking only for money damages.

Under Islamic law, however, criminal offenses are divided into two categories. The first category entails all offenses that are committed against the physical person of another individual (i.e., homicide and battery, *see infra*). This category partially coincides with the general theory of tort jurisprudence under the common law. However, Islamic law does not recognize tortious conduct such as false imprisonment, intentional infliction of emotional distress, or libel, slander, and defamation as creating a private cause of action. The second category entails all offenses that are committed against God. Thus, it is important to note that the state or the people are not represented by a prosecutorial body. Rather, God carries out justice and exercises mercy through the prosecutorial body for offenses that are against His will and, thus, detrimental to the Islamic community.

In any case, both of these categories are mutually exclusive. For example, the right to prosecute or forgive an act of homicide lies solely with the victim's family. That is, the Islamic prosecutorial body may not intervene. On the other hand, for example, the right to prosecute or forgive a slanderer lies solely within the purview of an Islamic judge. Thus, the victim of the slander may not sue the slanderer for damages.

There are three basic criminal offense categorizations under Islamic criminal law. However, when these offenses are committed, the *Shari'a* recognizes certain defenses that wholly remove culpability in addition to aggravating and mitigating factors that can allow for an increase or decrease in punishment.

B. CATEGORIZATION OF OFFENSES

Criminal offenses can be divided into three categories under Islamic law: *quesas*, *hudud*, and *tazir* offenses.

1. *Quesas* offenses

Both homicide and battery are qualified as *quesas* offenses under Islamic law. First, homicide is the intentional or unintentional killing of another human being. Next, battery is an intentional or unintentional act that causes permanent and serious bodily injury to another human being.

Quesas is an Arabic word that translates as "equality." As such, *quesas* crimes can be punished according to the principle of *lex talionis*. That is, the same injury which the defendant inflicted on the victim can be inflicted on the defendant in retaliation. Thus, an individual convicted of murder can be sentenced to death, while an individual convicted of causing

110

another to lose a limb can be punished by having her same limb amputated. However, the victim or her family can, in lieu of this physical punishment, demand *diyyah* (blood money) as compensation for the act or forgive the defendant entirely.

The legality of crime and punishment according to the *quesas* principle is found in both primary sources of Islamic law. It is enumerated in the *Qur'an* and confirmed in the *Sunnah*. Specifically, the *Qur'an* states,

> [a]nd We ordained for them therein a life for a life, an eye for an eye, a nose for a nose, an ear for an ear, a tooth for a tooth, and for wounds is legal retribution. But whoever gives [up his right as] charity, it is an expiation for him. And whoever does not judge by what Allah has revealed - then it is those who are the wrongdoers.[34]

2. *Hudud* offenses

Hadd is an Arabic word that means "fixed." Notwithstanding some minor disagreements, there are at least six *hudud* offenses under Islamic law. If the elements of the crime are strictly satisfied, each *hadd* offense calls for a unique fixed punishment according to standards laid down by the Prophet Muhammad (PBUH) in the *Qur'an* and *Sunnah*. The six common *hudud* offenses consist of theft, prohibited sexual intercourse, slander / defamation, highway robbery, apostasy, and consumption of intoxicants. However, the *Maliki fiqh* holds that rebellion is a *hadd* offense as well.

a. *Theft*

A person commits the *hadd* offense of theft when she intentionally takes property of value from the owner of the property without the owner's permission. The offense must

---

[34] *Qur'an* 5:45.

be proved by a confession or on the testimony of two male witnesses. However, one male witness can be substituted for two females. It is important to note that necessity is a valid defense to the crime of theft. The defense of necessity requires the existence of an imminent threat of danger; further, the defendant must have exhausted all legitimate means to confront the threat before committing the theft. If all of the elements for theft are proved, and if the defendant has no valid defense, then the fixed punishment for a conviction of theft is amputation of the right hand. A subsequent conviction of theft is punishable by amputation of the left foot.

b. Prohibited sexual intercourse

According to Islamic law, sexual intercourse is only permitted within the bounds of marriage. Thus, any sexual activity outside of marriage is a *hadd* offense. This includes fornication, adultery, and rape. An individual commits fornication if he or she is unmarried and engages in sexual intercourse with anyone. However, an individual commits adultery if he or she is married and engages in sexual intercourse with anyone other than his or her spouse. Finally, rape, for purposes of Islamic law, occurs when an individual engages in nonconsensual sexual intercourse with another individual outside the bounds of marriage. However, it is important to note that only the rapist, and not the victim, is subject to the fixed punishment for engaging in prohibited sexual intercourse. In any case, Islamic law does not recognize the crime of marital rape.

A *hadd* offense of engaging in prohibited sexual conduct must be proved in court by either a voluntary confession uttered by the accused or by eyewitnesses, subject to certain requirements for witness credibility (*see infra*). If the accuser seeks to prove the offense by eyewitness testimony, she must call four male eyewitnesses to testify.[35] However, one male eyewitness can be substituted for two female eyewitnesses. In any case, a conviction for committing a prohibited sexual act based on eyewitness testimony requires that each of the eyewitnesses testify to having seen the actual deed of sexual penetration.

Differences exist regarding the fixed punishment for engaging in prohibited sexual conduct. According to the *Qur'an*, which is the primary source of law under the *Shari'a*, the fixed punishment for a conviction of prohibited sexual conduct is flagellation. However, the defendant must not die from the punishment and must not receive more than 100 lashes.[36]

However, some commentators argue that there are certain accounts in the *Sunnah* that qualify this rule by creating a separate punishment for adultery (i.e., when a married individual engages in sexual intercourse with someone other than his or her lawful spouse). For example, one *hadith* states, "A man committed fornication with a woman. It was not known that he was married. So he was flogged. It was then known that he was married, so he was stoned to death."[37] Further, another *hadith* notes that a man came to Muhammad and admitted four times to committing prohibited sexual conduct. Muhammad turned the man away after each confession, except:

---

[35] "And those who accuse chaste women and then do not produce four witnesses - lash them with eighty lashes and do not accept from them testimony ever after. And those are the defiantly disobedient." *Qur'an* 24:4.

[36] "The woman or man found guilty of sexual intercourse - lash each one of them with a hundred lashes, and do not be taken by pity for them in the religion of Allah, if you should believe in Allah and the Last Day. And let a group of the believers witness their punishment." *Qur'an* 24:2.

[37] *Sunan* Abi Dawud, Book 40, *Hadith* 89.

when he had confessed four times, [the Prophet] ordered that he should be stoned. When he was being struck with the stones, he ran away, but a man caught up with him who had a camel's jawbone in his hand; he struck him and he fell down. The Prophet was told about how he fled when the stones hit him and he said: 'Why did you not let him be?'[38]

However, opponents of stoning as punishment for prohibited sexual conduct note that these accounts are questionable, that they pertain to very specific circumstances, and that Muhammad never condoned stoning as a fixed punishment for adultery in all cases. Thus, for the avoidance of doubt, these commentators argue that the *Qur'an* should prevail and the punishment of flagellation only should be applied for all convictions of prohibited sexual conduct, including fornication, adultery, and rape. Unfortunately, some Islamic law jurisdictions and radical groups, in total contravention of the Holy *Qur'an*, have even applied the questionable stoning punishment on persons convicted of fornication, rather than adultery.

c. Slander / defamation

Specifically, this *hadd* offense only applies to situations where the defendant falsely accuses another of prohibited sexual conduct or sexual abnormality. The fixed punishment for this *hadd* offense is flagellation with 80 lashes.[39]

The policy behind this offense reflects the overall policy of crime and punishment of *hudud* offenses in general. That is, the fixed punishments for *hudud* offenses are indeed severe which, thus, creates a very effective deterrent for would-be

---

[38] *Sunan* Ibn Majah Vol. 3, Book 20, *Hadith* 2554.

[39] "And those who accuse chaste women and then do not produce four witnesses - lash them with eighty lashes and do not accept from them testimony ever after. And those are the defiantly disobedient." *Qur'an* 24:4.

criminals. At the same time, the evidentiary requirements for proving *hudud* offenses are stringent, which means that very few perpetrators will actually be subjected to punishment. However, the threat of severe punishment is generally enough to deter most people from committing a *hadd* offense.

In the same way, the criminalization of the *hadd* offense of false accusation of prohibited sexual conduct has the effect of preventing punishment for prohibited sexual conduct in all but the most egregious circumstances. As aforementioned, the *hadd* offense of engaging in prohibited sexual relations must be proved by the testimony of four male witnesses, with the exception that one male witness can be substituted for two female witnesses. In any case, if only three witnesses give testimony accusing someone of engaging in adultery, or if the testimony of all four witnesses is defeated by overwhelming evidence, there is a possibility that all of the witnesses will be convicted of falsely accusing the defendant. Thus, together, these *hadd* offenses have the effect of discouraging prohibited sexual relations while encouraging witnesses to be extremely forthright when making serious allegations. However, witnesses to prohibited sexual relations do not necessarily have to take the wrongdoers to court immediately upon witnessing the misdeed. Rather, they can first confront them individually for surely no earthly punishment can be compared to the punishment for sin in the hereafter.

d. Highway robbery

In the most basic sense, highway robbery entails the use or threat of force to rob or attempt to rob travelers on a public conduit. During pre-Islamic times – and even today – law enforcement officials could not monitor every portion of the highway and, indeed, the risk of danger increased with the remoteness of urban centers. Given these factors, the harshness of punishment for attempted or completed highway robbery under the *Shari'a* is understandable.

However, the severity of the punishment is proportionate to the severity of the actual crime committed. Specifically, there are four subcategories of highway robbery which are punishable by increasingly severe sanctions.

- First, attempted robbery on the highway – which consists of only a confrontation without actually committing robbery – is punishable with banishment.

- Second, for actual robbery on the highway which results in physical harm to the victim, the fixed punishment is amputation of the opposing limbs (e.g., right hand and left foot).

- Third, for attempted robbery on the highway and homicide committed in furtherance thereof, the fixed punishment is death by the sword.

- Finally, the harshest punishment for highway robbery is crucifixion if the perpetrator both commits an actual robbery on the highway and commits homicide in furtherance thereof.

In the context of the nascent stage of Islam in the Arabian Gulf, highway robbery was a serious offense that, while involving only a limited amount of people, affected the safety, security, and survival of the entire community. That is, in order for trade and commerce to occur at a viable cost between regional groups, merchants and transporters must be guaranteed a certain amount of assurance that their goods and persons will be safe on the road.

This reality continues to exist today. An increase in danger and unrest in transporting people and goods inevitably results in a higher cost for the transportation, which is passed on to the price of the product. If left unpunished, merchants may conclude that the costs and risks associated with transporting their goods through dangerous territory outweigh the economic benefits of selling them within other regional areas. This could lead to a situation where urban centers lose access to necessary goods and services altogether. Thus, the severity of the fixed punishments for highway robbery serves to deter people from forming bandit gangs to take advantage of travelers at the cost of economic growth and freedom of movement.

e. Consumption of intoxicants

Several passages in the *Qur'an* and many teachings in the *Sunnah* proscribe consuming intoxicants for its deleterious effects on individual and societal harmony. These prohibitions forbid both the consumption of intoxicating substances, usually wine, as well as being in the state of intoxication. Today, it is clear that drugs and other illicit substances that provide little benefit other than to produce a state of intoxication are also prohibited. However, pharmaceutical drugs that are used to treat illness or mitigate pain are not necessarily forbidden if an intoxicated state occurs as a side effect to their ingestion.

To begin, there is no universal agreement regarding the fixed punishment that is required for committing the act of ingesting prohibited intoxicants resulting in a state of intoxication. According to some Islamic schools of law, the punishment is flagellation with 80 lashes. However, other schools hold that the punishment is flagellation with only 40 lashes.

The *hadd* offense of ingesting a prohibited intoxicating substance resulting in a state of intoxication must be proved on the testimony of two male witnesses. However, one male witness may be substituted for two female witnesses. Further, the persons who testify must meet all qualifications to serve as witnesses (*see infra*).

f. Apostasy

Under a common contemporary meaning, the act of apostasy means turning away from and denying a formerly held religious belief. Specifically to the *Shari'a*, apostasy is the renunciation of any of the main principles of Islam or conversion from Islam to another religion. At the outset, this presents a problem of interpretation due to the many sects and belief systems within Islam. That is, many *Sunni* Muslims would vociferously argue that *Shi'a* Muslims are apostates due to certain differences in their belief systems, while many *Shi'a* Muslims would strongly argue the reverse.

However, the Merriam-Webster dictionary provides a different definition of apostasy that applies outside of a religious realm. Namely, this alternate meaning defines apostasy as "abandonment of a previous loyalty; defection." While many extremists and fanatics would likely disagree, it is within this non-religious context of treason against the nascent Islamic State that the *hadd* offense of apostasy most likely applies.

Specifically, the early Muslim community and the Islamic State were subjected to significant outside oppression and attack.[40] From a practical perspective, the nascent Islamic State could not afford the disloyalty of even one Muslim follower, as this could indicate a sign of weakness in the community to both internal and external enemies, which could trigger massive defection and, eventually, the total destruction of Islam. It is with this context in mind that many modern Islamic scholars have interpreted the handful of passages in the *Sunnah* that provide for the possibility of corporal punishment for apostates. One such passage, as recorded by Muhammad Al Bukhari, states,

---

[40] *See infra* Chapter Seven for an expanded discussion of the Islamic State.

Allah's Messenger said, 'the blood of a Muslim who confesses that none has the right to be worshipped but Allah and that I am His Apostle, cannot be shed except in three cases: in *Quesas* for murder, a married person who commits illegal sexual intercourse, and the one who reverts from Islam and leaves the Muslims.'[41]

However, this passage does not explicitly set out a fixed punishment of a physical nature for apostasy. Indeed, it only implies that an apostate *may* be physically punished. Further, shedding the blood of an apostate is by no means a fixed punishment. Shedding blood could entail anything from a slight scratch on the skin to death.

It is important to note that nothing in the *Qur'an* suggests or requires that apostates from Islam be punished. Thus, the *Sunnah*, which is subordinate to the Holy *Qur'an*, is the only source in Islamic law that suggests that apostasy is a *hadd* offense. Despite the murkiness and disagreement surrounding this topic, the general belief is that apostasy is punishable by death for a male and imprisonment and flagellation for a female. However, a male apostate should be given three days prior to execution in which he is allowed to recant and return to Islam with no consequences. Further, the female apostate may recant and return to Islam at any time with no consequences

However, as the Islamic State is non-existent today, the need to make treason / apostasy punishable is also non-existent. Further, the *Qur'an*, which is the primary source of law and overrides the *Sunnah*, contains significant elements that support total freedom of religion. Indeed, one of the most oft-quoted passages of the *Qur'an* by Islamic reformists and liberals states "there is no compulsion in religion."[42] The

---

[41] *Sahih* Al Bukhari, Book 87, *Hadith* 17.
[42] *Qur'an* 2:256.

content of this passage would seem to negate any claim that religious freedom is prohibited under Islam. Further, another Quranic verse states,

> those who believed and those who were Jews or Christians or Sabians[43] - those [among them] who believed in Allah and the Last Day and did righteousness - will have their reward with their Lord, and no fear will there be concerning them, nor will they grieve.[44]

Further, another series of verses state,

> say, 'O People of the Book [Jews, Christians, and Sabians], you are [standing] on nothing until you uphold [the law of] the Torah, the Gospel, and what has been revealed to you from your Lord.' And that which has been revealed to you from your Lord will surely increase many of them in transgression and disbelief. So do not grieve over the disbelieving people. Indeed, those who have believed [in the Prophet Muhammad] and those [before him] who were Jews or Sabians or Christians - those [among them] who believed in Allah and the Last Day and did righteousness - no fear will there be concerning them, nor will they grieve.[45]

The basic underlying concept of Islam is submission to Allah, the God of Abraham. While the *Qur'an* and *Sunnah* clearly state that Islam is the best way to submit oneself to God, thereby achieving salvation, these passages also repeatedly affirm that there are other acceptable ways to submit oneself to the one true God (i.e., the God of Abraham). That is, Islam does not necessarily contradict Judaism, Christianity, and any

---

[43] The Sabians were followers of a monotheistic religion that worshipped the Abrahamic God.

[44] *Qur'an* 2:62.

[45] *Qur'an* 5:68-69.

other religion that worships exclusively the God of Abraham. As such, the existence of apostasy as a *hadd* offense is questionable.

g. Rebellion?

Only the *Maliki* school of jurisprudence regards rebellion as a *hadd* offense. As discussed later in Chapter Seven, rebellion against a legitimate Islamic governmental regime can be considered a *hadd* offense under Islamic law. A "legitimate" regime is basically one that was chosen by the public, has a generally reputable character, and is in compliance with the tenets of Islam. For those who claim that rebellion is one of the *hudud* offenses, the fixed penalty is death, whether on the battlefield or after a trial.

3. *Tazir* offenses

Tazir is an Arabic word that means "discretionary." As such, all offenses that undermine the Islamic social institutions of the Muslim community, yet cannot be categorized as a *hadd* or *quesas* offense, are subject to a discretionary punishment at the decision of a competent judge.

a. Three purposes

The *tazir* category of crime acts as a catchall provision under Islamic criminal jurisprudence. However, *tazir* as a catchall offense can be divided into three subcategories: deficient *hudud* and *quesas* offenses, indeterminately punished offenses, and all other offenses against Islam.

i. Deficient *hudud* and *quesas* offenses

A *tazir* punishment can be ordered when one or more necessary elements of a *hadd* or *quesas* offense cannot be proven, yet there is strong evidence that the accused committed the act and should be punished. For example, a defendant can be subject to a discretionary punishment for attempted murder, attempted battery, attempted theft, and so on. In the same manner, if, for example, the accuser can only procure half of the required witness testimony required to prove a certain offense, and if the judge believes that the procured testimony is sufficiently strong, the accused can be subjected to a lesser *tazir* penalty.

ii. Indeterminately punished offenses

Islamic law specifically proscribes certain activities that are deemed to be damaging to the individual and the community without denoting a specific punishment for carrying out such activities. For example, the *Qur'an* states repeatedly, and all other sources of law confirm, that engaging in usurious activities as well as gambling is forbidden. However, the law does not provide a specific punishment for these actions. Thus, a judge has discretion to order a *tazir* punishment when such forbidden, yet indeterminately punished offenses are proven in court.

iii. Offenses against Islam

Recall in Chapter One the secondary sources of law, which include *Qiyas* (analogical reasoning), *Ijma* (consensus), and *Ijtihad*, as well as the *hadith* which narrates Muhammad as saying "[m]y community will not agree upon error."[46] The primary sources of law (the *Qur'an* and *Sunnah*) are regarded as both divine and timeless. Yet, they were formulated around 1,400 years ago, when the modern technology and living standards that prevail today were nonexistent. As such, any offense which is not specifically forbidden in the text of the primary sources of law can be punished with a *tazir* penalty if the offense is deemed to contravene the overarching principles of Islam.

---

[46] *Sunan* Ibn Majah, 2:1303.

For example, lust of the flesh and carnal temptation are disapproved in Islam. Indeed, the *Qur'an* states,

> tell the believing men to reduce [some] of their vision and guard their private parts. That is purer for them. Indeed, Allah is acquainted with what they do. And tell the believing women to reduce [some] of their vision and guard their private parts and not expose their adornment except that which [necessarily] appears thereof and to wrap [a portion of] their headcovers over their chests and not expose their adornment.[47]

Thus, it can be inferred that producing, distributing, or viewing pornography is against the overarching principles of Islam. Hence, engaging in such activity can be subjected to a *tazir* punishment.

b. Punishment

Tazir offenses can be punished with, for example, banishment, imprisonment, a monetary fine, flagellation, amputation, or death, depending on the severity of the offense. However, it is important to note that rehabilitation is one of the main goals of punishment under the theory of *tazir*. Thus, severe punishments such as death are only ordered in extreme circumstances.

Notwithstanding the foregoing, the predominant view of Islamic legal scholars is that the discretionary punishment for a deficiently proved *hadd* or *quesas* offense brought as a *tazir* offense must be less severe than the punishment prescribed for the relevant *hadd* or *quesas* offense. That is, the punishment for the *hadd* offense of fornication is flagellation by no more than 100 lashes. Thus, a *tazir* penalty for a deficiently proven charge of fornication – for example, where the accuser could only find half of the required witnesses – must be less severe

---

[47] *Qur'an* 24:30-31.

than the punishment of flagellation with no more than 100 lashes.

C. AGGRAVATING AND MITIGATING FACTORS; DEFENSES

Islamic law recognizes that, in some situations, punishment should be increased, decreased, or withheld altogether based on certain factors and characteristics that an offender may possess. Further, the *Shari'a* recognizes that committing an otherwise evil act is justified at certain times due to compelling circumstances.

First, while the punishment for committing an offense can be increased on the basis of a convicted defendant's lack of remorse, recidivism, or on other aggravating factors, the punishment can be lessened or forgiven altogether based on certain mitigating factors. In this scenario, the offender is clearly guilty of committing a wrongful act, but the circumstances may allow for a lesser punishment. That is, all elements of the crime have been satisfied and proven in court either as a *hadd* offense or *tazir* offense, but the judge may deem that, for example, the offender was acting under the influence of uncontrollable rage. However, it is important to note that this concept only applies to offenses committed against and enforced by the public. In *quesas* offenses (*see supra*), inflicting punishment or granting forgiveness on the guilty party is entirely at the discretion of the private parties involved.

On the other hand, some circumstances excuse an otherwise unlawful act based on permissibility. That is, all of the elements of the offense have been sufficiently proven and the defendant may have even admitted to committing the act, but due to certain factors, the defendant should not be held guilty for committing the act. Most often, an otherwise guilty party can be held innocent when the defendant lacked volition to commit the act, was mentally insane, was acting in self-defense or defense of property, and in other circumstances.

1. Lack of volition

When an individual commits an unlawful act without the free will to commit the act, she cannot be held guilty. An individual lacks the volition to commit an act when, for example, she is unconscious, intoxicated, or under the influence of duress.

An individual cannot be held liable for acts committed while sleeping or while otherwise unconscious. In the same way, an individual cannot be held liable for acts committed while under the influence of intoxicating substances. However, intoxication is not a defense in the case of willingly consuming alcohol or an illicit substance. That is, acts committed while under the influence of intoxication caused by ingesting duly prescribed and beneficial medication which causes a side effect of intoxication cannot give rise to a guilty conviction. However, when an individual willingly ingests substances that are unlawful and prohibited under Islamic law, any resulting intoxication cannot absolve the individual of subsequent wrongful acts.

When an individual commits an act under duress, she is not acting of her own free will. Rather, she is acting according to the will of an external force. In order to prove the defense of duress, the defendant must show that: 1) there was a credible threat that coerced the defendant to commit the act; 2) the defendant had an actual, subjective fear that the threat would be carried out; and 3) the threatening party had the ability to carry out the threat. When an individual commits an act under duress, she cannot be held guilty of any resulting harm.

2. Insanity

Mental insanity refers to a condition wherein the defendant was unable to distinguish between right and wrong or good and bad at the time of the offense. For example, assume that a defendant truly believed that she was chopping down a tree with an axe when, in fact, she was striking her neighbor with the axe. The defendant cannot be held liable for any resulting injury or death because her mental insanity at the time of the offense is a defense to the otherwise wrongful act.

3. Self-defense and defense of property

An individual may not be held liable for acts committed to prevent a crime against her person or property. However, using physical force in this circumstance is only allowed as a defense to an otherwise unlawful act when the force was used to repel aggression. Further, an individual who uses this defense to justify an otherwise unlawful act must prove that it was impossible to rely on the protection of a police force at the time of the act.

4. Other causes for permissibility

Islamic law recognizes that many otherwise unlawful acts should not be punished under the criminal law or create a private cause of action due to various factors. For example, an employee cannot be held liable for certain harmful acts that she committed within the scope of her employment. Furthermore, harm that results from inherently dangerous conduct does not give rise to liability under Islamic law. For example, if an individual receives an injury while playing a sport, she cannot seek retaliation nor can the offender be guilty of a *tazir* offense.

Also, the family is considered a largely autonomous entity under Islamic law and the governing authorities rarely interfere with family dynamics. Under Islamic family law (*see supra* Chapter Five), men have a right to physically punish their wives in certain extreme circumstances. Further, parents have the duty to raise their children correctly as well as the right to receive respect and obedience from their children. As such, men cannot be punished for disciplining their wives when done so in the appropriate circumstances according to the *Shari'a*. Further, parents cannot be punished for using physical discipline against their children. In this same vein, children are not liable for their wrongful acts. Generally, children do not reach an age of criminal liability for their actions until the age of seven years or upon puberty.

D. CRIMINAL PROCEDURE AND INVESTIGATIONS

When physical evidence is required to prove an accused party guilty of a crime, governmental forces must carry out investigations and gather the necessary physical evidence. In any jurisdiction, there is a tension between the desire of the individual for liberty and autonomy and the desire of the public for safety and justice. At times, the nature of the investigation and evidence gathering processes requires the infringement of individual privacy in order to sufficiently and accurately carry out justice. This ability to infringe upon individual liberty, autonomy, and privacy is an awesome power indeed and is, thus, subject to governmental abuse if left unchecked.

For this reason, a hallmark of human dignity and respect encapsulated in the legal systems of many civilized nations is the right to live peacefully and privately, free from interference and prying by government forces. For example, the Fourth Amendment of the U.S. Constitution provides,

> [t]he right of the people to be secure in their persons, houses, papers, and effects, against unreasonable searches and seizures, shall not be violated, and no

Warrants shall issue, but upon probable cause, supported by Oath or affirmation, and particularly describing the place to be searched, and the persons or things to be seized.

In addition to the home, the U.S. Supreme Court has found that this right of security and freedom from government interference in one's daily affairs extends to any place where an individual has a reasonable expectation of privacy.[48] In both state and federal criminal investigations in the U.S., the Fourth Amendment is most effectively enforced with the implementation of the Exclusionary Rule, which requires that unconstitutionally obtained evidence be suppressed in the prosecution's case against the accused.

Similarly, Islamic law recognizes the autonomy of the individual, the family, and the home and forbids arbitrary governmental prying and intermeddling in such areas. For example, one *Sunnah* account records Muhammad as saying, "[a]nyone who listens to people's conversation when they move away from him will have molten lead poured into his ears."[49] Furthermore, the *Qur'an* states,

> O you who have believed, do not enter houses other than your own houses until you ascertain welcome and greet their inhabitants. That is best for you; perhaps you will be reminded. And if you do not find anyone therein, do not enter them until permission has been given you. And if it is said to you, 'Go back,' then go back; it is purer for you. And Allah is knowing of what you do.[50]

Similar to the Fourth Amendment, this Quranic passage forbids arbitrary trespass into the home. However, this passage seemingly affords a higher degree of protection to

---

[48] Katz v. United States, 389 U.S. 347 (1967).
[49] Al Adab Al Mufrad, Book 47, *Hadith* 1159.
[50] *Qur'an* 24:27-28.

individual autonomy in the home than does the U.S. Constitution because permission from the homeowner, which can be withheld, is required to gain entry. On the other hand, a warrant to enter a private dwelling can be obtained without the homeowner's consent under the Fourth Amendment simply by receiving permission from a judge or magistrate.

While the desire for justice and public safety is no less important in Islamic law jurisdictions than in any other jurisdiction, the permissibility of the means of gathering physical evidence for use at trial is different. This distinction, perhaps, stems from the theistic roots in Islam. That is, in secular jurisdictions, justice is considered a wholly earthly concept, with mankind's governmental establishments maintaining the sole responsibility for investigations, proof, and punishment. In the religious framework of the *Shari'a*, however, God sees all and has exclusive power to inflict punishment or exercise mercy both here on earth and in the hereafter, regardless of mankind's establishments and desire for justice. Thus, perhaps the need for extensive gathering of physical evidence at the cost of individual privacy is not as pressing a concern under Islamic law.

E. TRIAL PROCEDURE AND EVIDENCE

An accusation of a criminal offense cannot be acted upon until the act has been proved in court before an Islamic judge. Importantly, there is no right to a jury trial under Islamic law, but the judge hearing the case must be impartial and fair throughout the trial. In addition to physical evidence, an accusation of a criminal offense can be proved with witness testimony as well as a confession from the accused. However, Islamic law places constraints on these forms of evidence when used at trial.

1. Witness testimony

Testimony of a witness is admissible to prove a criminal offense. However, the admissibility of the evidence is dependent upon the characteristics of the witness. First, the witness must be mentally sound both at the witnessing of the alleged crime as well as at trial. That is, she must have the mental capacity to understand the questions which she is asked at trial and her memory must be absolutely clear regarding the event. In this regard, it is generally required that the witness experienced both the visual and audial components of the alleged crime. That is, blindness and deafness is usually sufficient to disqualify a witness from testifying. Furthermore, a person who is mute may not serve as a witness, even by writing or gesturing her testimony. The reason for this stems from the strict requirement that witnesses utter the oath "ash-hadu" – which means "I testify" in Arabic – prior to giving testimony. This oath triggers a serious obligation on the witness to speak with complete and utter truthfulness and entails severe earthly and eternal consequences for breaching.

Next, a witness must be Muslim in order for her testimony to be admissible. Further, she must have a generally reputable character without any record of criminal activity. In this regard, the witness may not be an enemy of the defendant and there must not be any hostility between them. Furthermore, the witness must not be a family member of any of the parties involved.

Finally, when a specific amount of witnesses is required to prove a certain offense, two qualifying female witnesses may substitute for one male qualifying witness. However, the testimony of minors is usually inadmissible, notwithstanding gender.

2. Confessions

The use of an accused's confession can be sufficient to prove a criminal offense. However, the admissibility of a confession is dependent upon the characteristics of the accused and the manner in which the confession was extracted. First, a confession must be made voluntarily in order to be admissible. That is, a confession made under duress or while mentally unsound is inadmissible. Further, a confession may not be extracted through the use of mental or physical torture. In this regard, a confession to a criminal act is only valid if it is made in court in front of a qualified Islamic judge.

Next, the confession must be clear, detailed, and unequivocal. According to the *Hanafi fiqh*, verbal utterance of the confession is required. Further, the clear and unequivocal details contained within the confession must be corroborated by the facts of the case. Finally, a minor's confession is invalid.

CHAPTER 7. LAW OF WAR

A. INTRODUCTION

Armed conflict and the necessity of using deadly military force are inevitable occurrences in an imperfect world. Islamic law provides much guidance regarding the purposes, methods, and justifications for carrying out such activities, perhaps because of the context in which the primary sources of Islamic law were formed. Indeed, Islam was born in a time of significant conflict and chaos in the Arabian Gulf which occurred as a result of misunderstandings, miscommunication, and retaliatory attacks between warring familial groups. Thereafter, the Prophet Muhammad (PBUH) and the first Muslims faced religious persecution and oppression on the basis of their beliefs and teachings. However, as Islam began to spread – first in Medina, then to Mecca and to all other parts of the Middle East – the followers of Islam began to obtain the upper hand in number and strength such that the Islamic community, rather than the unbelievers, was capable of oppression.

The law of war under the *Shari'a* encompasses justifications for the use of military force as well as rules that govern how military force may be used and how non-Muslim conquered persons should be treated. However, before engaging in an analysis of the law of war under the *Shari'a*, it is important to note that the sources of Islamic law must be studied rigorously within the context of their inception. One cannot fully understand the content of a religious text without first understanding its context. For this reason, it is important to understand the concepts related to statehood and enemy identification under Islamic law at the outset.

1. Islamic statehood

To begin, the Islamic law of war mainly concerns the protection and propagation of the Islamic State. Muhammad first established the Islamic State in Medina and presided over it as supreme ruler. However, when Muhammad died, the Muslim community was faced with the dilemma of choosing a leader to fill his position and govern the Islamic State. Thus, the post-Muhammad Islamic State is a Caliphate ruled by a single Caliph who governs the entire Islamic community much in the way that Muhammad did (keeping in mind that Muhammad is considered the final Prophet and messenger of Allah).

When Muhammad died, the Islamic community disagreed on choosing a successor. One sect believed that the title of Caliph should be bestowed on someone chosen by the people and the companions of Muhammad (the *Sunni* sect), while another sect believed that the title of Caliph should pass through the bloodline of Muhammad (the *Shi'ite* sect). The *Sunni* sect elected a close friend of Muhammad, Abu Bakr, as Caliph. However, the *Shi'a* believed the cousin and son-in-law of Muhammad, Ali ibn Abu Talib, was the rightful successor and refused to recognize Abu Bakr as Caliph. Thus, arguably the Islamic State was dissolved immediately upon the death of Muhammad because the Islamic community was divided, with two different sects recognizing two different leaders as legitimate. However, most scholars agree that the Islamic State was perpetuated by the Rightly Guided Caliphs of the Rashidun Caliphate up until the year 661.

Eventually, the *Shi'a* leader Ali ibn Abu Talib was elected Caliph and acted as the final leader of the Rashidun Caliphate. Thereafter, most scholars agree that the Islamic State was dissolved due to significant disagreement and strife within the Islamic community. However, some believe that the Islamic State, though somewhat disorganized, was still intact. Nevertheless, without the guidance of Muhammad, each successive Caliph had to look to his consultative council as well as the sources of Islamic law to effectively govern the Islamic community while remaining faithful to the tenets of Islam. Inevitably, as each successive Caliphate became more removed from the time of Muhammad's life, their practices also became less and less similar to the model of governance carried out by Muhammad.

Arguably, Abdul-Mecid II was the final Caliph, and the Ottoman Empire the final Caliphate, of Islam. However, many scholars and laypeople alike believe that most, if not all, of the Caliphs and Caliphates that followed the Rashidun Caliphate were illegitimate in whole or in part. The arguments for this position point to the un-Islamic characteristics of the successive Caliphates including, for example, the manner in which leaders attained and retained their titles as well as the way that they governed.

Today, it is widely agreed that the Islamic State no longer exists. This concept introduces a tension in the application of Islamic law, especially in the field of international relations and specifically with regard to the law of war. To be sure, there are many Islamic states whose governments are wholly or partially influenced by Islam. These independent states can have confidence in applying Islamic law in their courts with regard to purely internal matters involving, for example, contracts, marriage, criminal actions, and so on. However, when these independent states engage in international relations, the application of Islamic law is less clear because they are acting in their own interests, not in the interests of the entire Muslim population.

In this regard, one can see why the vast majority of Muslims today denounce the actions of such persons and groups as Osama bin Laden, Al Qaeda, the Taliban, Al Shabab, and even the Muslim Brotherhood, who have invoked Islam in justifying violence. First, these actors lurk in the shadows in even the most devout Muslim countries and attract a tiny minority of fanatics. Only a legitimate ruler of the entire Muslim community can declare war or order military action to be carried out in defense of Islam. Thus, such shadowy and fragmented terrorist organizations do not act on behalf of the Muslim community and have no legitimate power to carry out military action on behalf of any purported Islamic State. Furthermore, terrorist organizations today use certain tactics that are wholly contrary to Islamic law including, for example, intentionally targeting civilian non-combatants (*see infra*).

Thus, it is important to keep in mind the tension involved in applying principles of Islamic international law in today's world. For this reason, some scholars hold that all of Islamic international law is wholly inapplicable today because there is no Islamic State with a centralized body led by a Caliph. However, other scholars say that some principles of Islamic international law are binding on Islamic peoples and governments today. Thus, the applicability of the law of war under the *Shari'a* in today's rapidly changing world is subject to wide debate.

2. Enemy identification

With the concept of the Islamic State and its current limitations in mind, it is important nonetheless to note that, under Islamic law, the entire population of the world is divided into two theoretical spheres of influence. The Islamic State and all lands under its control is referred to as the "place of peace" (*dar al Islam*). On the other hand, all unconquered lands and all territories governed by a non-Muslim authority lie within the "place of war" (*dar al harb*). The distinction between these two spheres of influence is important in determining, for example, when military force is justified, against whom such force justified, and how such force may be carried out.

B. JUSTIFICATION FOR WAR

War and military aggression are only allowed in the place of peace in order to quell an unjustifiable rebellion, liberate the people from an illegitimate ruler, or repel an outside attack as an act of self-defense. In the same way, war and military aggression are allowed in the *dar al harb* in certain circumstances that justify using offensive force.

1. War within the *dar al Islam*

Because the *dar al Islam* is presumptively ruled in accordance with the principles and tenets of Islam, it should have the characteristics of justice, order, and peace. However, this is not always the case. War is justified in the *dar al Islam* when repelling an outside attack from an external enemy or when quelling an unjustified rebellion. On the other hand, war is justified in certain extreme circumstances to liberate the Islamic people residing in the *dar al Islam* from an illegitimate Caliph.

a. *Self-defense against an external attack*

An attack against the place of peace committed by outside forces of the *dar al harb* is considered to be an attack on Islam. That is, it is not just an act of physical aggression against human beings with purely tangible and concrete ramifications. Rather, it is considered to be an attack on the intangible and abstract concept of Islam that is meant to destroy the message and hope for salvation contained therein. As such, the use of force in defending the Islamic State is justified, if not required, to repel an outside attack on the *dar al Islam*.

b. Armed force in internal uprisings

As a purely internal matter, the concept of uprisings in the *dar al Islam* under the *Shari'a* may be more suited to Islamic criminal law rather than the law of war. In any case, there are two concerns for determining when the use of military force is justified in an internal uprising. The first concern deals with a situation wherein the Islamic people initiate a civil war in order to liberate itself from an illegitimate Caliph. The second concern deals with a situation wherein the legitimate Islamic authority uses military force to quell an unjustified rebellion.

i. Liberation

First, civil war is justified in the *dar al Islam* in extreme circumstances when Muslims residing therein take up arms against an illegitimate authority. However, in this circumstance, military force should be a last resort after all peaceful means of seeking justice or a change in leadership have failed. Many scholars hold to the broad view that the Islamic authority is legitimate so long as it is fully compliant with Islam. Generally, therefore, when all peaceful means to remove an authority that is in contravention of Islam have failed, a civil war initiated by the Muslim people to remove the authority is justified.

ii. Rebellion

On the other hand, when the Islamic authority is in compliance with Islam, taking up arms against it in rebellion is unjustified. That is, rebellion in order to seize power on behalf of an individual or familial or tribal group is unjustified. Further, rebellion solely on the basis of a Caliph's incompetence is also unjustified. In this circumstance, the people would first have to seek the peaceful removal of the incompetent ruler. If such peaceful removal fails, only then would a civil war be justified. Therefore, when Muslims residing in the *dar al Islam* engage in an unjustified rebellion, the Islamic authority is allowed to use force to repel the attack, quell the rebellion, and reinstate order in the *dar al Islam*.

2. War in the *dar al harb* – offensive force

Offensive military force refers to a situation wherein Islamic forces under the direction and control of the Islamic State engage in war in the *dar al harb* against non-Muslim forces. However, the Islamic State is only justified in engaging in an offensive war in one specific circumstance.

At the outset, it is important to note that nothing in Islamic law authorizes the Islamic State to use offensive force solely for the purpose of acquiring land or spreading Islam. However, that is not to say that the Islamic State and its citizens are not interested in bringing their message of salvation to all people of the world. Rather, the sole interest in engaging in offensive war is to protect the Islamic State so that it can continue to expand.

While land-grabbing and swordpoint conversions are not appropriate justifications for offensive war, as the territory and influence of the Islamic State expands such that Muslim citizens residing in the *dar al Islam* begin to come into systematic contact with non-Muslim citizens of the *dar al harb*, the Islamic State is permitted to continue its expansion. However, the expansion of the ideals of Islam and the Islamic State is likely to be weakened or undermined by the presence of autonomous non-Muslim groups residing within the territory of the Islamic State, who may engage in an uprising or attempt to convert Muslims from Islam. Thus, when the territory and influence of the Islamic State expands such that Muslim citizens residing in the *dar al Islam* begin to come into systematic contact with non-Muslim citizens of the *dar al harb*, the Islamic authority must present the non-Muslim citizens with three choices: 1) convert to Islam; 2) reject Islam and pay *jizyah* (a tribute tax, *see infra*); or 3) reject Islam, refuse to pay *jizyah*, and go to war.

Any non-Muslim who chooses to convert to Islam immediately becomes a full citizen of the Islamic State with all resulting rights and privileges. However, non-Muslims who refuse to accept Islam but choose to pay *jizyah* – such persons are called *ahl al dhimma* (people of the subjugation treaty) or *dhimmis* – are subject to certain restrictions and are granted certain rights (*see infra*). For example, a *dhimmi* is restricted in her ability to openly practice her religion. However, the *ahl al dhimma* must be protected in both their physical, religious, and legal capacities while under Islamic control.

On the other hand, if any non-Muslim citizens within the territory that lies in the path of the expanding Islamic State both refuse to pay the tax and refuse to accept Islam, then the Islamic State is justified in waging an offensive war against them. In this scenario, as in all other circumstances where war is justified, it is important to understand the rules that Islamic law mandates for carrying out military force (*see infra*).

C. RULES CONTROLLING HOW WAR IS CARRIED OUT

As aforementioned, Islamic law justifies military action in the *dar al Islam* in order to quell an unjustifiable rebellion, liberate the people from an illegitimate ruler, or repel an outside attack as an act of self-defense. Further, war and military aggression are allowed in the *dar al harb* in one particular circumstance. In any situation, when war is justified, Islamic law sets out certain limits and requirements for carrying out aggressive, physical force. The use of military force under the *Shari'a* takes into account the religious identification of combatants as well as the principle of distinction in relation to the treatment of non-combatants during war.

1. Self-defense against an external attack

In the case of military action in self-defense to repel an attack launched by non-Muslim forces against the whole of the Islamic State, the paramount objective according to the *Shari'a* is the protection of the Islamic State and its citizens. An attack on the Islamic State is deemed to be an attack on Islam and its entire message of salvation. Frankly, therefore, it would seem that any means necessary to achieve that objective is theoretically permissible.

However, it is important to note that force used in self-defense is limited to defense only and does not encompass offensive force. Military action in this realm often leads to discussions that inevitably culminate in pointing to a slippery slope argument, namely, where does one draw the line on self-defense? Or, when does defensive action become offensive? For example, if non-Muslim military forces cross into Muslim territory, is the Islamic State limited to only driving the enemy out of the established territory of the Muslims, or is it permitted to pursue the enemy throughout the lands under non-Muslim control until each soldier, aider, and abettor is subdued? In the former instance, the actions of the Muslim forces would seem to perhaps fall short of effective self-defense in that the receding non-Muslim forces could regroup behind the border and launch another offensive invasion whilst the Muslim military forces turn to depart from the border and return home. In the latter instance, however, there is a danger of overzealousness in trampling on the land of non-Muslims who may have had nothing to do with the aggression.

Perhaps the best guidance in this scenario can be found in the most important source of Islamic law, which states

> [i]f you [people] have to respond to an attack, make your response proportionate, but it is best to stand fast. So [Prophet] be steadfast: your steadfastness

141

comes only from Allah. Do not grieve over them; do not be distressed by their scheming, for Allah is with those who are aware of Him and who do good.[51]

This passage implores Muhammad and the Muslim community to first stand fast in the face of offensive force, instead of carrying out an immediate act of retaliation. However, when defensive force is necessary, this passage requires that it be carried out in proportion to the initial act of aggression. Further, the *Qur'an* states,

[f]ight in the way of Allah those who fight you but do not transgress the limits. Indeed. Allah does not love transgressors.[52]

Thus, the *Shari'a* condones the limited use of military force in self-defense if it is carried out in proportion to the initial act of aggression.

2. Rebellion

As aforementioned, for purposes of this book, rebellion refers to the unlawful uprising against a legitimate authority. In the case of an internal rebellion, Islamic criminal law sets out fixed punishments for specific crimes, called *hudud* offenses (*see supra* Chapter Six). The *Maliki* school of thought in Islamic law holds that rebellion is a *hadd* offense that is punishable by death. However, all other schools hold that rebellion is a separate offense that calls for a discretionary punishment, which can be lessened or excused altogether depending on the convicted rebel's reasons for engaging in the act. In any case, if any rebels retreat or surrender during a rebellion, they are to be arrested only and not killed. Put differently, retreating Muslim rebels who are nevertheless in the wrong for their actions should not be stabbed, shot, or otherwise attacked in the back whilst running away. Rather,

---

[51] *Qur'an* 16:126 - 128.
[52] *Qur'an* 2:190.

all effort should be made to capture and try the rebels in a court setting.

3. Offensive force

As aforementioned, nothing in Islamic law necessarily advocates territorial expansionism solely for the sake of acquiring land and regional clout. Rather, the overarching purpose behind the expansion of the Islamic State is best expressed in intangible terms at a religious level, rather than on an earthly level. That is, the goal of every Muslim individually and the Islamic State collectively is to be submitted to the will of God. In turn, God's will is that all people live in peace on earth. However, peace is often difficult to achieve between two or more autonomous groups with their own religious teachings and viewpoints, especially in the nascency of Islam when communication and understanding between such groups was difficult. In this sense, the Muslim forces can wage war on non-Muslim groups in the *dar al harb* that stand in the way of the expansion of the Islamic State and refuse to convert or pay the subjugation tax. However, there are limits to the use of force that may be carried out in this context.

First, anyone who is a Muslim residing in non-Muslim territory is not considered an enemy and is to be protected from aggression and intentional targeting. Next, Islamic law prohibits targeting and killing any woman, child, or elderly person during war, regardless of religious affiliation or willingness to pay the subjugation tax. Put differently, in an offensive war, all non-Muslim males are presumed to be enemy combatants and only non-Muslim males may be targeted. Thus, in the face of military conflict, all non-Muslim males are subject to death. However, the practices of the Islamic State under Muhammad and successive Caliphs have traditionally excluded certain neutral individuals – including slaves, traveling merchants, and any other person who does not pose a reasonable threat – from this category.

D. TREATMENT OF PRISONERS OF WAR AND *AHL AL DHIMMA*

Whenever an armed altercation occurs between the Islamic State's military forces and an external force, the non-Muslim group can always cease hostilities and agree to either convert to Islam or pay the *jizyah*. If the non-Muslim people group agrees to submit to the Islamic State and pay *jizyah*, the two parties will enter into a subjugation treaty (*dhimma*) which grants each party certain rights and imposes on each party certain duties. The *Shari'a* sets out the relationship that will exist between the Islamic State and the subjugated group. Nevertheless, when conflict occurs, each side of the conflict will generally capture enemy prisoners of war, either during hostilities or afterward. Islamic law sets out the rules in relation to the treatment of prisoners of war.

1. Prisoners of war

During and after an armed conflict, Muslim forces will likely capture non-Muslim prisoners of war. These persons must be dealt with according to certain restrictions under the *Shari'a*. As a general rule, all prisoners of war can be set free, enslaved, or exchanged for Muslim prisoners of war held by the enemy.

However, adult male prisoners of war can be executed at any time due to their status as a combatant who has refused to convert to Islam or pay *jizyah*. On the other hand, adult female prisoners of war and slaves can be taken as wives by Muslim men. When this occurs, it is generally accepted that all formalities, rights, and duties of the marriage contract apply to both parties (*see supra* Chapter Five). For example, the *Qur'an* states, and [also prohibited to you are all] married women except those your right hands possess. [This is] the decree of Allah upon you. And lawful to you are [all others] beyond these, [provided] that you seek them [in marriage] with [gifts from] your property, desiring chastity, not unlawful sexual intercourse. So for whatever you enjoy [of marriage] from them, give them their due compensation as an obligation.[53]

In any case, the Muslim authority has wide discretion, subject only to the *Shari'a*, to choose how prisoners are dealt with once war is over.

While in the custody of a Muslim, a prisoner of war must be treated humanely. For example, the *Qur'an* states, "[the righteous] give food in spite of love for it to the needy, the orphan, and the captive, [saying], 'we feed you only for the countenance of Allah. We wish not from you reward or gratitude.'"[54] In the same way, slaves must be cared for and treated well while in the possession of a Muslim master. For example, Islam admonishes to "do good to . . . orphans, the needy, the near neighbor, the neighbor farther away, the companion at your side, the traveler, and those whom your right hands possess."[55]

With this in mind, it is important to note that enslavement is not necessarily meant to be a permanent condition for conquered non-Muslims. Indeed, freeing a captive person or slave is considered to be a righteous and honorable act. For example, the *Qur'an* states,

righteousness is [in] one who believes in Allah, the Last Day, the angels, the Book, and the prophets and gives wealth, in spite of love for it, to relatives,

---

[53] *Qur'an* 4:24.
[54] *Qur'an* 76:8-9.
[55] *Qur'an* 4:36.

orphans, the needy, the traveler, those who ask [for help], and for freeing slaves.[56]

Further, freeing a slave is commanded in some scenarios as atonement for sin that has been committed.[57]

2. *Ahl al dhimma*

As aforementioned, citizens of the *dar al harb* who are in the path of the Islamic State's expansion are subject to three choices: 1) convert to Islam and become a full citizen of the Islamic State with all concomitant rights and privileges; 2) reject Islam and pay *jizyah*; or 3) reject Islam, refuse to pay *jizyah*, and go to war.

When non-Muslims choose to reject Islam but, instead, accept subjugation and pay *jizyah*, they will enter into a treaty with the Islamic State called a *dhimma*. Certain freedoms of the *ahl al dhimma* (people of the *dhimma*) are restricted under the treaty. In turn, the Islamic State must recognize and protect certain rights held by each *dhimmi* under subjugation.

a. *Restrictions under the* dhimma

Essentially, subjugated persons living under a *dhimma* treaty must agree to pay *jizyah*, which is a tax paid as tribute, as evidence of their willingness to abide by the treaty and in return for certain rights and protections granted by the Islamic State. However, the *dhimmi*s are also restricted in their behavior in certain circumstances.

---

[56] *Qur'an* 2:177.

[57] *See, e.g., Qur'an* 5:89 ("Allah will not impose blame upon you for what is meaningless in your oaths, but He will impose blame upon you for [breaking] what you intended of oaths. So its expiation is [*inter alia*] . . . the freeing of a slave."); *see also, e.g., Qur'an* 58:3 ("[a]nd those who pronounce [divorce] from their wives and then [wish to] go back on what they said - then [there must be] the freeing of a slave before they touch one another. That is what you are admonished thereby; and Allah is Acquainted with what you do.").

i. *Jizyah*

First, *jizyah* is a per capita tax collected on all able-bodied males living under a *dhimma* treaty. That is, the *jizyah* tax is set at a fixed amount, as opposed to *Zakat*, which is collected at 2.5 percent of a Muslim's wealth. Throughout Islamic history, the fixed amount to be paid as *jizyah* has varied substantially from time to time. However, some leaders increased the amount for wealthier *dhimmi*s and lowered it for poorer *dhimmi*s. In any case, women, children, and the elderly were exempted from the obligation to pay the tax.

However, it is important to note that many Islamic leaders collected the *jizyah* tax in a lump sum from the leader of the *dhimmi*s instead of going door to door and collecting the tax individually from each able-bodied male. Most often, for example, if there were one thousand able-bodied males living in a people group under a dhimma treaty and the *jizyah* was set at 25 dirhams each, then the leader of the *dhimmi*s would be expected to turn over 25,000 dirhams to the Islamic State at the prescribed period. The manner in which the leader collected the required amount was of no concern to the Muslim authority. Thus, the leader of the *dhimmi*s could institute and collect a tax on every *dhimmi* in order to satisfy the *jizyah*.

Finally, the funds paid as *jizyah* become the property of the Muslim citizens of the Islamic State and should be used by the Islamic authorities to fund public institutions such as the military, mosques, schools, hospitals, and roads. However, it is important to note that the *dhimmi*s benefit from these public institutions as well. For example, while the *dhimmi*s do not have to enlist and fight in the Muslim army, they receive the protection of the Islamic State's military forces against external attacks (*see infra*).

ii. Other restrictions

While *dhimmi*s are permitted to live under their former religious rules, the practice of their religious beliefs that conflict with the principles of Islam must be carried out in private and away from the possible view of Muslims. For example, praying to Jesus or Mary can only be done in private. Further, the public display of non-Muslim religious symbols such as crosses or idols is forbidden. In the same way, any form of proselytization to Muslims is forbidden since it is unlawful for Muslims to commit the *hadd* offense of apostasy under the *Shari'a*.

Furthermore, *dhimmi*s are permitted to engage in non-religious activities that are contrary to the principles of Islam. However, the activities must be carried out in private and must not be forbidden by the religious law of the *dhimmi*s. For example, *dhimmi*s are not forbidden from consuming alcohol and pork under Islamic law. Further, engaging in adultery or fornication carries with it a discretionary punishment for *dhimmi*s, while Muslims are subject to the more severe fixed punishment.

Finally, *dhimmi*s are forbidden from holding important positions in the Islamic State's government structure. For example, a *dhimmi* cannot serve as a judge in an Islamic court. Further, a *dhimmi* cannot serve as a witness in any legal matter in which a Muslim citizen has an interest.

b. Rights under the dhimma

While subjugation carries with it a negative connotation, the *dhimma* relationship between a non-Muslim people group and the Islamic State is not without benefits. Indeed, throughout much of Islamic history, subjugation under the Islamic State actually provided many non-Muslims with an increase in the quality of life and a greater recognition of human rights than that which they experienced prior to subjugation.

First, *dhimmi*s are permitted to hold and practice their own religious beliefs and govern themselves according to their own religious laws. However, if a Muslim is involved in a dispute with a *dhimmi*, then the dispute may be brought before an Islamic judge and decided according to Islamic law. Generally, *dhimmi*s and Muslim citizens are supposed to be regarded as equal before the law in an Islamic court. This reality is most prevalent in the economic realm. Specifically, *dhimmi*s are entitled to be treated equally with regard to most legal transactions undertaken with a Muslim party. For example, a contract entered into between a *dhimmi* and a Muslim must be executed in the same manner as any other contract and afforded the same judicial protection as if both parties were Muslims. That is, an Islamic judge is not permitted to issue a ruling in favor of a Muslim party to a dispute brought by a *dhimmi* simply because of the *dhimmi*'s status as a subjugated person.

However, in certain situations that occur between a *dhimmi* and a Muslim, Islamic law may allow for the dispute to be decided in a way that is favorable to the Muslim party. For example, one Islamic school of law, the *Hanafi fiqh*, holds that *dhimmi*s and Muslims are accorded equal status under the *quesas* principle of crime and punishment. Specifically, when a Muslim kills a *dhimmi*, the *Hanafi fiqh* holds that the rights of the slain *dhimmi*'s family are equal to that of a Muslim. That is, the slain *dhimmi*'s family has the option to order that the Muslim who committed the homicide be killed in retaliation. However, all other schools of law state that a Muslim may never be killed in retaliation for the homicide of a *dhimmi*. This majority view is drawn from several *ahadith,* one of which states, "[a] believer should not be killed in retaliation for the murder of a disbeliever."[58]

While Islamic law can be interpreted in such a way that the right of retaliation for the *quesas* offense of homicide is restricted for *dhimmi*s, most other criminal law provisions treat Muslims and *dhimmi*s equally. For example, if a Muslim batters a *dhimmi* by causing permanent bodily injury, the victimized *dhimmi* has the full right of retaliation against the offender. Further, if a Muslim commits theft against a *dhimmi*, the offender is still subject to the *hadd* punishment of amputation of the right hand, regardless of the victim's lesser status.

Finally, it is important to note that *dhimmi*s benefit from the full protection of the Islamic State's military resources under the *dhimma* treaty. Further, the *dhimmi*s are not required to fight in any armed conflicts or otherwise enlist in any military force while under the Islamic State's control. At the same time, Islamic forces are required to defend and protect the lives and property of *dhimmi*s from all external attacks.

---

[58] *Sunan* Ibn Majah, Vol. 3, Book 21, *Hadith* 2660. *See also Sunan* Abu-Dawud, Book 39, Number 4491.

APPENDICES

GLOSSARY

Adverse possession A legal doctrine that provides for transfer of title to land by way of possessing it. Generally, in addition to any statutory requirements, the possession must be actual, visible, open and notorious, exclusive, under claim of ownership, hostile, and continuous.

Ahl al dhimma An Arabic phrase meaning the people of the *dhimma*.

Counterofferor One who has rejected an offer made by an offeror and makes a counteroffer.

Dar al harb An Arabic phrase meaning the place or abode of war. Land that is not under control of the Islamic State.

Dar al Islam An Arabic phrase meaning the place or abode of peace. Land that is under control of the Islamic State.

Dhimmi An Arabic word meaning a non-Muslim living within land controlled by the Islamic State and under a subjugation treaty.

Diyyah An Arabic word meaning blood money. Money paid to a victim or a victim's family in compensation for battery or homicide.

Easement The right to use or control another's property for a specific purpose.

Fiqh Islamic jurisprudence; Islamic school of legal thought.

Fuqaha The plural form of *fiqh*.

Gharar An Arabic word meaning excessive risk or uncertainty. A prohibited contractual element.

Halaal An Arabic word meaning permissible, lawful, legal.

Hadd An Arabic word meaning fixed. A criminal offense that, when proved, is punishable with a specific penalty.

Hudud The plural form of *hadd*.

Iddat An Arabic word meaning waiting period. The waiting period that a woman must undergo after divorce or the death of her husband before she can remarry. The waiting period for a divorced woman is three menstrual cycles or until she gives birth. The waiting period for a widow is generally four months and ten days.

Ijara An Arabic word meaning lease. A permissible financial instrument.

Jizyah An Arabic word meaning subjugation tax. The subjugation tax collected on adult male non-Muslims living under a *dhimma* treaty.

Khul'a An Arabic word meaning compensational divorce. A manner in which a woman may seek divorce from her husband by offering compensation, usually expressed in terms of the woman's dowry.

Lex talionis A Latin phrase meaning law of retaliation. The right of a physically injured party or her family to inflict equal physical damage on the offender.

Mahr An Arabic word meaning dowry.

Majlis An Arabic word meaning meeting or joining together.

Mudaraba Sleeping partnership. A permissible financial instrument whereby an investor offers capital to an investee in return for a percentage of profit earned by the investee's use of the capital.

Murabaha Markup and resale agreement. A permissible financial instrument whereby an investor purchases an asset and resells it to a borrower at a marked up price to be paid in regular installment payments.

Nafaka An Arabic word meaning maintenance. The duty of a husband and father to provide food, clothing, and shelter to his wife and children according to his earning capacity.

Nisab The threshold amount of income that an individual must meet in order to be liable for *Zakat*.

Offeree One who receives an offer.

Offeror One who makes an offer.

Pledge A debtor's act of offering property to a creditor as security for a loan. If the loan is not repaid, the creditor may have recourse to the property.

Possession The use or control of property. Possession can be held with or without holding title to the property.

Quesas An Arabic word meaning equality. An offense that causes physical injury or death and creates a right in the victim or the victim's family to seek compensation in the form of blood money or retaliation by inflicting the same injury on the offender.

Riba An Arabic word meaning usury or unjust enrichment. A prohibited contractual element.

Stare decisis A doctrine that encourages adherence to legal interpretations and principles laid down in previous judicial rulings. The phrase literally means "to stand by things decided" in Latin.

Sukuk An Arabic word meaning legal instruments. A tradable certificate evidencing a right to receive payments from an investee.

Talaaq An Arabic word meaning divorce. Specifically, it is a man's right to revoke his marriage. *Talaaq* may not be exercised by a woman.

Talaaq ahsan The most favorable method of divorce.

Talaaq bid'ee The most disapproved method of divorce.

Talaaq hasan A method of divorce that is neither favorable nor unfavorable.

Tazir An Arabic word meaning discretionary. A criminal act that is neither a *hadd* nor a *quesas* offense, yet is subject to a discretionary punishment.

Title The right to own, sell, mortgage, or otherwise control or alienate property.

Waliemah An Islamic tradition consisting of a post-nuptial meal provided to the community by both families of a new marriage.

Zakat One of the Five Pillars of Islam. A tax on Muslims generally calculated at 2.5 percent of cash income, 5 to 10 percent of agricultural income, and 20 percent of income received by extracting natural resources or minerals from the earth.

ORGANISATION OF ISLAMIC COOPERATION (OIC) MEMBER STATES

OIC MEMBER STATE	AFFILIATION OF MUSLIM POPULATION
Afghanistan	*Sunni* majority, but large *Shi'a* population.
Albania	*Sunni* majority.
Algeria	*Sunni* majority.
Azerbaijan	*Shi'a* majority.
Bahrain	*Shi'a* majority.
Bangladesh	*Sunni* majority.
Benin	*Sunni* majority.
Brunei	*Sunni* majority.
Burkina Faso	*Sunni* majority.
Cameroon	*Sunni* majority.
Chad	*Sunni* majority.
Comoros	*Sunni* majority.
Côte d'Ivoire	*Sunni* majority.
Djibouti	*Sunni* majority.
Egypt	*Sunni* majority.
Gabon	*Sunni* majority.
Gambia	*Sunni* majority.
Guinea	*Sunni* majority.

Guinea-Bissau	*Sunni* majority.
Guyana	*Sunni* majority.
Indonesia	*Sunni* majority, but large *Shi'a* population.
Iran	*Shi'a* majority.
Iraq	*Shi'a* majority.
Jordan	*Sunni* majority.
Kazakhstan	*Sunni* majority.
Kuwait	*Sunni* majority, but large *Shi'a* population.
Kyrgyzstan	*Sunni* majority.
Lebanon	*Sunni* majority, but large *Shi'a* population.
Libya	*Sunni* majority.
Malaysia	*Sunni* majority.
Maldives	*Sunni* majority.
Mali	*Sunni* majority.
Mauritania	*Sunni* majority.
Morocco	*Sunni* majority.
Mozambique	*Sunni* majority.
Niger	*Sunni* majority.
Nigeria	*Sunni* majority, but large *Shi'a* population.
Oman	*Ibadi* majority.
Pakistan	*Sunni* majority, but large *Shi'a* population.
Palestine	*Sunni* majority.
Qatar	*Sunni* majority, but large *Shi'a* population.
Saudi Arabia	*Sunni* majority, but large *Shi'a* population.

Senegal	Sufi majority.
Sierra Leone	*Sunni* majority.
Somalia	*Sunni* majority.
Sudan	*Sunni* majority.
Suriname	*Sunni* majority.
Syria	*Sunni* majority, but large *Shi'a* population.
Tajikistan	*Sunni* majority.
Togo	*Sunni* majority.
Tunisia	*Sunni* majority.
Turkey	*Sunni* majority, but large *Shi'a* population.
Turkmenistan	*Sunni* majority.
Uganda	*Sunni* majority.
United Arab Emirates	*Sunni* majority.
Uzbekistan	*Sunni* majority.
Yemen	*Sunni* majority, but large *Shi'a* population.

ABOUT THE AUTHOR

Jonathan G. Burns (J.D., Indiana University Robert H. McKinney School of Law, 2014; B.A., Evangel University, 2010) is the author of *The Banking Sector in Post-Revolution Egypt: Is Islam the Solution?*, Banking and Finance Law Review, Volume 29 Issue 2 (2014) and *Just War Theory: The Perspectives of Christianity, Islam and Modern International Law Compared*, 2013 Emerging Issues 7050 (LexisNexis, 2013) (co-author).

Jonathan has lived and worked in the Kingdom of Saudi Arabia. At the Robert H. McKinney School of Law, he studied Islamic and international law and sat on the Editorial Board for the Indiana International & Comparative Law Review. Contact the author by writing to: JonathanBurns@TellerBooks.com.

CPSIA information can be obtained at www.ICGtesting.com
Printed in the USA
BVOW04s2214050914

365762BV00001B/37/P